PRACTICAL
Art
SCHOOL

WATERCOLOUR
PAINTING

WATERCOLOUR
PAINTING
GERALD WOODS

WATERCOLOUR PAINTING

A LITTLE, BROWN BOOK

Designed, written and edited by
THE BRIDGEWATER BOOK COMPANY LTD

First published in Great Britain in 1995
by Little, Brown and Company

CLB 4070
© 1994 COLOUR LIBRARY BOOKS LTD
Godalming, Surrey
The moral right of the author has been asserted.

A CIP catalogue record for this book
is available from the British Library

ISBN   0 316 91274 3

10 9 8 7 6 5 4 3 2 1

Designed by Peter Bridgewater / Annie Moss
Edited by Viv Croot
Managing Editor Anna Clarkson
Photography by Jeremy Thomas
Typesetting by Vanessa Good / Kirsty Wall

Colour separation by Scantrans PTE Ltd, Singapore
Printed and bound in Spain by Graficas Estella

Little, Brown and Company (UK) Ltd
Brettenham House
Lancaster Place
London WC2E 7EN

Contents

At-A-Glance Guide

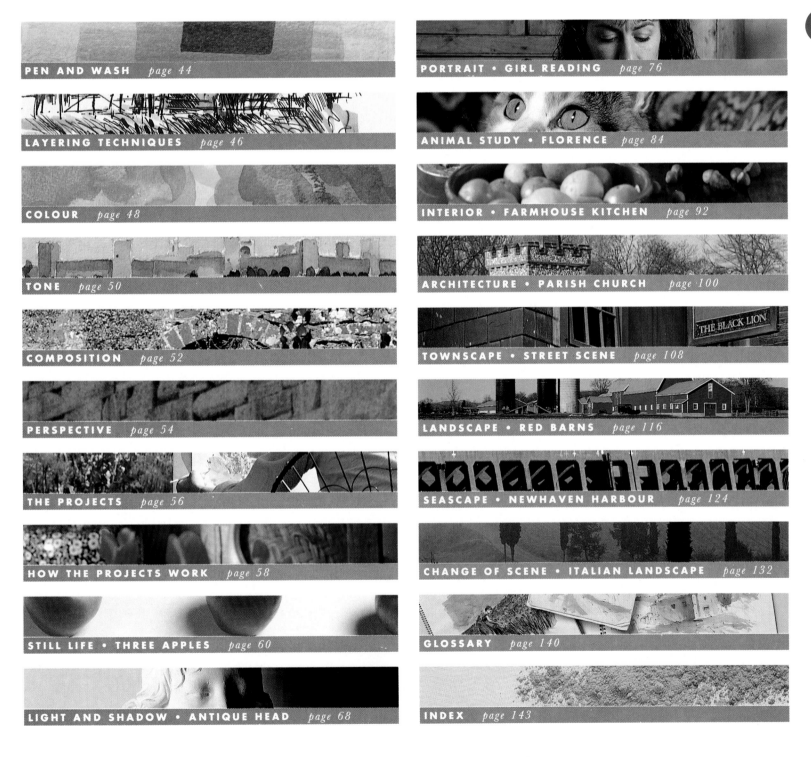

Introduction

Having shaken off the image of being a 'polite hobby' for genteel Victorian ladies, watercolour is now generally regarded as a medium capable of serious artistic expression. For many people the whole activity of painting in watercolour is a process which is analogous to nature itself. The layering of translucent washes over one another is akin to the order of natural growth. Unconsciously perhaps, many artists working in watercolour are attempting to produce paintings which can be enjoyed in the way that one enjoys real fields, trees and meadows. The love of landscape is one of the most deeply felt of human sentiments and this, in part, accounts for the renewed interest in watercolour.

Watercolour is an ideal medium for recording the many moods and momentary effects of light in landscape, as Turner demonstrated so magnificently in his studies of mountains, lakes and rivers. Of course, one need not be confined to landscape as a subject – as is evident in the range of themes and examples in the Project Section of this book.

The artist is always in a learning situation – after a lifetime of painting landscapes from direct observation, Paul Cézanne confided to his friend Emile Zola, 'rather late – I have begun to see nature'. We learn from artists like Cézanne, we learn from different cultures, from different periods of art history and, when a group of like-minded individuals work together in an art class, they learn from one another.

In this book you will see how three different artists using watercolour interpret the same subject. An artist never paints things as they are, but as he or she sees them – and this, essentially, is what distinguishes the work of one artist from another. Because the exact reproduction of nature is an impossible pursuit, we tend to extract or select different things from whatever view confronts us. You will see, for instance, how the artists in this book working from the same still life will nevertheless interpret it differently. While one artist might be primarily concerned with the compositional relationship between objects, another might be more interested in colour, texture and tonal value. But at the end of a painting session, each can compare his or her interpretation with that of other people in the group and, inevitably, understanding of the subject is enhanced by the very differences of interpretation and visual expression.

Consciously or unconsciously, we 'borrow' ideas from one another. I might, for example, be impressed by the way in which another artist 'handles' or applies colour or by the particular quality of marks made with a brush or pencil. At one time an essential part of an artist's training was to visit the Louvre, the National Gallery or other such institutions, to make direct copies from master paintings. This is not to suggest that one should not be single-minded – the painter Gwen John, when asked if she admired the work of Cézanne, replied that she did, but that she liked her own work better! The point being that while we are able to learn from each other, we must at the same time try to discover the world in our own terms. Seeing is a search for meaning and understanding; for what matters most to an artist is not the nature of the world itself but the nature of his or her reactions to it.

The whole point of this book, therefore, is not just to help you gain a better understanding of the essential characteristics of the watercolour medium, but also to enable you to use it to say what *you* want to say.

MATERIALS
AND
TECHNIQUES

Choosing Materials

12

Just to see a profusion of artists' materials in an art store can be sufficient inducement to make you want to start painting straight away. Row upon row of shining new tubes of colour, paintboxes, brushes, sketchbooks and so on all combine to make you feel that, if only you possessed these things, you would be already halfway to being an artist!

But this, of course, is an illusion – watercolour paintings can be produced with a minimum amount of equipment. You can manage perfectly well with a paintbox containing a dozen colours, a few pencils, brushes and paper. What matters, however, is that the materials you do buy are of the best quality.

Watercolours, in particular, should be bought from an artists' colourman of repute – cheap substitutes usually contain chalk filler and other additives. Try to include at least one sable brush in your selection. Some of the brushes made from synthetic hair, however, are less expensive and quite good.

There are many watercolour papers to choose from but, in the first instance, avoid buying paper that is heavier than 190gsm / 90lb. Heavier papers are very expensive and you would feel inhibited about the possibility of making mistakes.

When working outside, you will want to avoid having to carry too much equipment. In the course of trying to find the right viewpoint for your painting, you may have to walk a considerable distance and climb to different levels. You will feel less inclined to do this if you are weighted down with equipment.

There are a number of lightweight sketching easels made from beechwood or aluminium, which can be folded and are easily carried. However, I would rather invest in a good lightweight folding chair, since to my mind it is just as easy to balance a sketchbook on my knee as to work at an easel.

A half-pan watercolour box. Both the lid and the fold-out palette can be used for mixing colour.

Sketch book, paints, brushes and all the sundry materials you will need can easily be carried in a small shoulder bag.

A BASIC KIT FOR LANDSCAPE PAINTING

● Sketchbook (preferably spiral-bound); alternatively, sheets of paper clipped to a lightweight board.

● A box of watercolours containing the following colours: *Cadmium Yellow, Yellow Ochre, Burnt Sienna, Burnt Umber, Alizarin Crimson, Cadmium Red, Indian Red, Payne's Grey, Cerulean Blue, Ultramarine, Monastral Blue and Lamp Black.*

● A ceramic mixing palette (an old saucer or plate will do).

● At least three brushes: a large wash brush No. 20 or a Hake, No. 6 sable for finer work, and a long haired 'rigger' for painting lines; a brush holder (see page 25) to carry them in.

● Pencils 2B or 3B and a knife (never use a pencil sharpener), rubber, pen and ink, Chinese White in a tube.

● A lightweight shoulder bag to carry everything in.

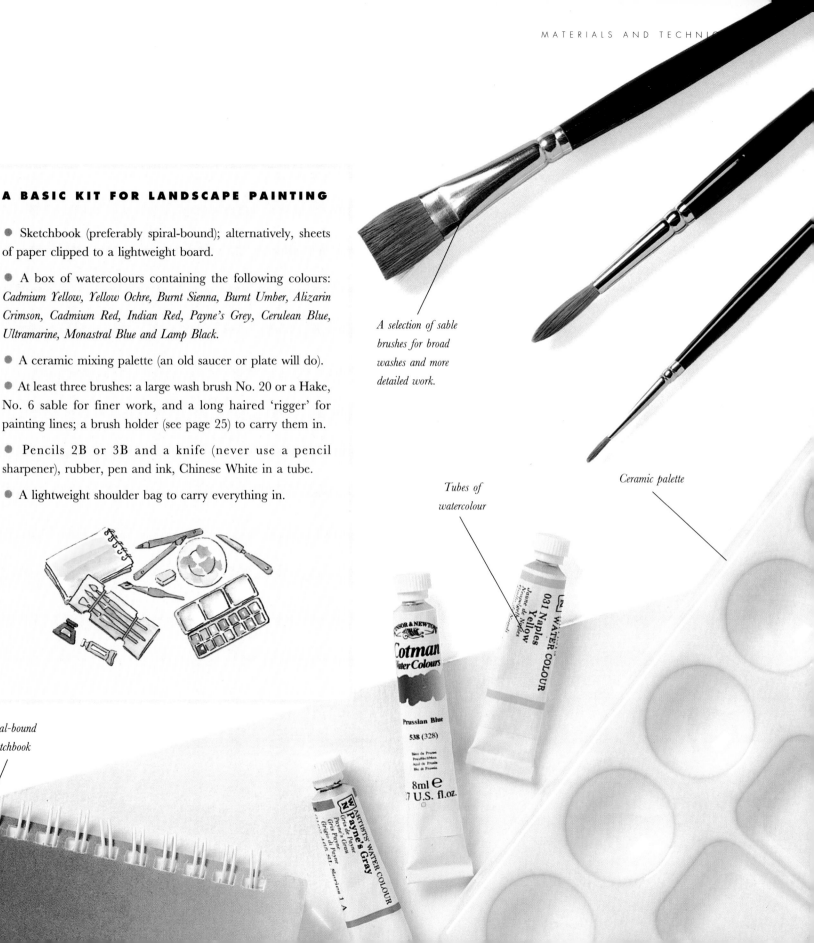

A selection of sable brushes for broad washes and more detailed work.

Tubes of watercolour

Ceramic palette

Spiral-bound sketchbook

Paper

A sized white paper is the support normally used for water-colour painting. The artist today is faced with a wide choice of papers from England, France, Italy and Japan.

My own preference is for paper which is not too heavily sized, and without a pronounced 'tooth'.

Arches, Saunders Waterford, Whatman and *Fabriano* are all fine papers which bring out the best characteristics of transparent water-colour glazes. In the first instance, however, any white paper which is heavy enough to withstand stretching, washing-out and re-working, and which does not buckle when wet, is ideal. Inexperienced artists should initially avoid expensive papers with a pronounced 'tooth', which might tend to flatter the work, and avoid toned papers for the same reason.

Watercolour papers are classified by weight and surface texture.

● CP/NOT (cold-pressed/not-pressed) has a semi-rough surface of medium grain which accepts washes without too much absorption.

● HP (hot-pressed) papers have a much smoother surface with a fine grain with sufficient texture to retain a wash. It is an ideal paper for working in pencil and wash or for fine brushwork.

● ROUGH paper has a coarse surface, achieved by drying the sheets between rough felts without pressing. This paper is most suited to strong, broadly-painted washes. It is generally unsuited to pen and ink or soft pencil, which tends to smudge.

WEIGHT

At one time, the thickness of paper was determined by the weight of a ream (500 sheets) of that particular paper in a given size. Today, however, it is expressed as the weight of a square metre of a single sheet of paper given in grammes – gsm. An average weight for a watercolour paper would be about 300gsm / 140lb. The heaviest is about 638gsm / 300lb.

SIZING

Watercolour papers are generally sized. Unsized papers, known as waterleaf, are generally unsuitable since they absorb the colour and tend to 'bleed'. The 'right' side of the paper is determined by the maker's name which appears as a watermark reading in the right direction when held up to the light.

Bockingford oatmeal
190gsm / 90lb (NOT)

BACKGROUND
Fabriano Rough
105gsm / 90lb

Bockingford cream
190gsm / 90lb
(NOT)

Bockingford eggshell
190gsm / 90lb (NOT)

Arches blanc
190gsm / 90lb (NOT)

Bockingford white
535gsm / 250lb (NOT)

Bockingford
300gsm / 140lb
(HP)

Saunders Waterford
300gsm / 140lb (HP)

Fabriano Artistico
300gsm / 140lb (HP)

Fabriano Rough Artistico
190gsm / 90lb (NOT)

Watercolour papers are usually sold as loose sheets, spiral or edge-bound pads, or in block form.

Sketchbooks

Sketchbooks are made in a great many shapes and sizes, from small pocketbooks to larger, more unwieldy sizes.

Constable was in the habit of using very small pocket sketchbooks which he always carried with him ready to draw anything that beckoned his attention. Bonnard, too, produced some of his most intimate drawings on the pages of an old diary. In a sense, a sketchbook is a visual diary in which one records everyday observations. Many sketchbooks conform to the 'A' Series, from A1 (594mm x 841mm / 23.39 inches x 33.11 inches) to A5 (148mm x 210mm / 5,83 inches x 8.27 inches).

The quality of the paper varies from an inexpensive machine-made cartridge to heavier weights of mould-made watercolour paper. It is now possible to buy a range of tinted Bockingford papers in the form of a spiral-bound sketchbook.

Alternatively, you may prefer to select a range of different papers and have them bound by a bookbinder. One advantage of doing this is that the paper can be cut to a proportion of your own choosing. It is rare, for instance, to find a sketchbook that is square in proportion.

More economically, you can simply sandwich a variety of papers between two stout sheets of cardboard or millboard, held together with fold-back metal clips.

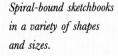

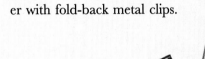

Spiral-bound sketchbooks in a variety of shapes and sizes.

Bockingford tinted (eggshell) 190gsm / 90lb CP (NOT) surface. This paper could be used as a base tint for a painting which employs predominantly cool tones – a seascape, for example.

Bockingford tinted (oatmeal) 190gsm / 90lb CP (NOT) surface. A useful paper for landscape subjects which are warm in tone.

Bockingford white 190gsm / 90lb CP (NOT) surface. A good general purpose paper which is acid-free and has found favour with watercolourists for its excellent paint removal properties.

Saunders Waterford
190gsm / 90lb 100%
cotton CP (NOT) gelatine
sized. This is a
premium quality paper
which is acid-free and is
available in 3 surface
finishes and 4 weights.

Fabriano Artistico
300gsm / 140lb
(ROUGH). An Italian
paper made from 100%
cotton. The raised
texture of this paper
calls for strong washes
and bold tonal content.

Aquarelle Arches
300gsm / 140lb
(NOT). Probably the
best paper for combining
pencil and watercolour –
the surface is not too
textured nor is it
heavily sized.

Paints

18

In the manufacture of watercolours the pigment is first separated into individual particles. Gum arabic, which comes from the acacia tree, is one of the most important additives, since it binds the pigment together and is also water-soluble. Because most pigments do not blend easily into aqueous solutions, other wetting agents are required, such as oxgall, and detergents to aid the process of dispersion. Sugar and glycerine are also added to prevent the colours from drying out completely.

Most manufacturers have jealously guarded their recipes and only one has been prepared to publish his formulae. The London colourman, Robert Ackermann, was able not only to offer sixty-eight prepared watercolours for sale in 1801, but also published the recipe for those who wished to prepare their own colours. Ackermann's recipe involved four separate stages of manufacture and included gum arabic, sugar candy, distilled water, honey and distilled vinegar in varying proportions. But he warned those who wanted to prepare their own colours that, 'the time, the trouble, the expense of attending their preparation will never compensate the small saving gained by it.'

Watercolours are usually bought as a pre-selected range of colours in the form of semi-moist cakes or pans, contained in a metal box. The compartmentalised lid of the box acts as a mixing palette when the box is opened out flat. Half-pans are small cakes of colour held in a plastic container 2 cm/³/₄ inches

square. You may, however, prefer to buy an empty colour box and select your own colours – in which case, you can mix half-pans with full-pans of colour. The full-pans are likely to be colours you will use most frequently – blues, yellows and reds – while your half-pans might be restricted to colours that are used sparingly, such as violet, Lamp Black or crimson.

Some artists prefer the convenience of having tubes of watercolour, or bottles of liquid watercolour. Much depends on the kind of work you are doing. If, for example, you are painting a landscape, then you might want to be able to see all your colours at a single glance without having to squeeze them out of individual tubes. On the other hand, you might consider it an advantage to be able to squeeze out just enough colour for your purpose.

When selecting your own colours, you will no doubt add some of the more unusual hues to the basic set of primary, secondary and tertiary colours. You might also be guided in your choice of palette by the colours used by the great watercolourists. Turner, for instance, used several Chrome Yellows, Cobalt Blue, Indian Red, Madder, Yellow Ochre, Vermilion, Venetian Red and Raw Sienna.

Tubes contain water-colour pigment in a more liquid form. The texture of the paint is generally more consistent than pan colours.

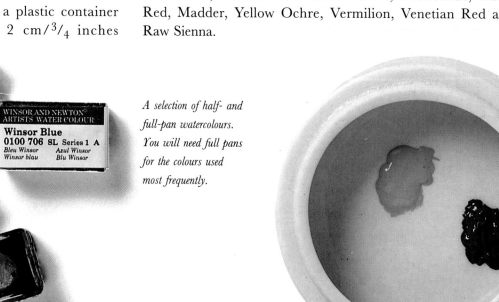

A selection of half- and full-pan watercolours. You will need full pans for the colours used most frequently.

19

The choice of colours will not, of course, in itself turn you into a good colourist – but it can be a contributing factor. It is important to choose watercolours of a good quality. Poor-quality watercolours usually contain too much white filler. You will only be able to reproduce rich, granular washes by using artists' quality paints.

Most manufacturers offer some guidance as to the permanence or fugitiveness of their colours. Alizarin Green is fugitive, and Prussian Blue is liable to fade. Vermilion darkens in bright light, and colours with a dye content, such as Alizarin Crimson, are difficult to remove.

You will discover that certain colours are better used in small patches than as large flat washes. Colours such as French Ultramarine, for instance, tend to granulate either alone or when mixed with other colours. The behaviour of different pigments will become more apparent with practice. Certain effects achieved by mixing colour may be unexpected and can either enhance a painting or ruin it altogether.

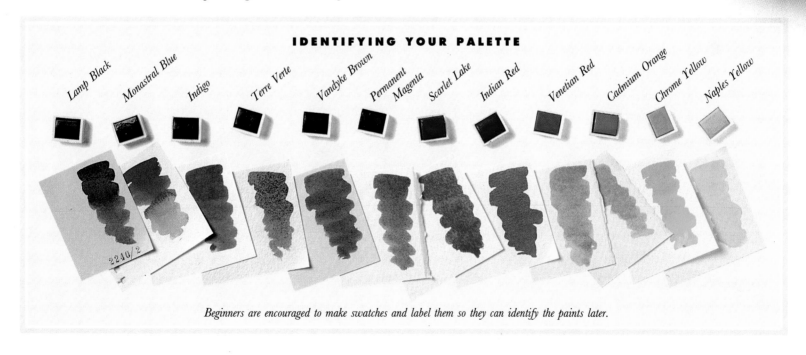

IDENTIFYING YOUR PALETTE

Lamp Black · Monastral Blue · Indigo · Terre Verte · Vandyke Brown · Permanent Magenta · Scarlet Lake · Indian Red · Venetian Red · Cadmium Orange · Chrome Yellow · Naples Yellow

Beginners are encouraged to make swatches and label them so they can identify the paints later.

Media

The quality of a watercolour painting can be enriched by combining various techniques and materials. Coloured inks, for instance, produce transparent glazes which are entirely different in character from a wash made with pure watercolour. Inks contain less pigment and are less absorbent. The opaqueness of gouache paint, which is heavily pigmented, can provide effective tonal contrast to the luminosity of watercolour. Tempera paints, which are water-soluble, have great permanency and can also be successfully combined with watercolour.

In the paintings of the late John Piper, one can see how effectively watercolour, gouache, pen and ink, coloured inks, pastel and wax resist can be combined. If exactly the kind of texture you want to produce can best be achieved by harnessing materials together in an unorthodox way, then you shouldn't worry too much about purist attitudes to watercolour. On the other hand, there is no great virtue in mixing media in the hope that it might help resolve problems that have more to do with fundamental weaknesses in the work as a whole.

Transparent coloured inks can be successfully combined with watercolour.

A 'self-sharpening' wax china marker pencil is used to produce a soft, grainy line.

Aquarelle pencils in different hues of blue can be used 'dry' or diluted with a wet brush.

All masking fluids dry within minutes and are easily rubbed off with fingers leaving no residue.

Tubes of gouache for opaque areas of colour.

A wax candle for creating a resist.

An old toothbrush to create spatter

A bamboo pen with a broad nib which produces a broad uneven line.

By experimenting with media and varying your painting techniques, you can achieve many different qualities in your work.

Paint Additives

GUM ARABIC/WATERCOLOUR MEDIUM

This is a mixture of gum arabic and acetic acid which acts as a binder and extender. It is particularly useful when working on top of several layered washes to prevent the colour sinking. Watercolour glazes can be enhanced by the addition of gum arabic

ABOVE *Diluted gum arabic. It can be mixed in varying proportions with watercolour pigment.*

RIGHT *An example of a brighter colour mixed with gum and laid over layered washes – notice how the colour retains its tonal strength.*

OXGALL LIQUID

This additive is available in 40, 100, 250, 500ml and litre sizes. It is generally used to improve the wetting and flow of watercolour paint. To improve the acceptance of watercolour on various papers, the liquid oxgall is diluted with water and used as a primer. It can also be mixed directly with the paint to produce a smoother flow of colour. Additionally, it can be used as a flat wash (with a touch of colour) over a finished painting to bring colours together tonally.

PREPARED SIZE

You may find a particularly attractive paper to work on which is too absorbent for watercolour. Prepared size is used to make the paper less absorbent. It should be warmed gently before use so that it is free flowing and can be brushed directly onto the paper and left to dry. Prepared size can also be useful as a base for wet-in-wet painting to prevent the colour from spreading too much.

LEFT *Colours applied wet-on-wet onto paper which has been sized by hand.*

VARNISH

If a watercolour is to be framed underglass, it is not really necessary to varnish the surface. There are, however, a number of paper varnishes made from synthetic resin dissolved in white spirit which the manufacturers claim do not affect the colour or tone of the painting.

RICE STARCH

Victorian watercolourists sometimes added fine powdered rice starch to the colour mix to produce a dry, pastel-like quality. In an age of aerosol sprays, rice starch is becoming increasingly difficult to find.

Pens & Pencils

A selection of pens

A selection of Graphite pencils 2B to 6B

23

The pen most commonly used in conjunction with watercolour is the traditional dip pen. It can be used with any type of ink and even with dilute paint. Metal nibs are manufactured not only for drawing, but also for lettering, calligraphy and technical drawing. There are, therefore, a wide variety to select from, ranging from fine mapping pens to broad-tipped lettering nibs. When choosing a nib, make sure that it is sufficiently flexible to enable you to draw without constantly having to re-charge with ink. Some nibs have brass reservoirs which retain more ink.

Goose and turkey quills are fairly easily obtained and can be cut to a fine drawing point. For a bolder, more expressive line, use a reed pen or a calligraphy pen. When working outside you can, in fact, make a reasonable drawing instrument by simply sharpening a twig or stalk which, when dipped in ink, will produce a dry broken line.

A good-quality pencil has a fairly high proportion of graphite in the lead to produce a smooth line. When using a pencil to work alongside watercolour (rather than as an underdrawing), use a medium-soft grade; B grades are soft and produce a more sensitive line than either H or HB. The surface texture of the paper used can also greatly influence the quality of line.

Aquarelle pencils are produced in a broad range of colours and are water-soluble. The marks made by these pencils can be dissolved and extended as a wash with a wet brush. Water-soluble graphite pencils are also now generally available.

Graduated tones produced by softening the marks made with Graphite Aquarelle pencils with a brush and water.

Homemade Bamboo and Reed pens and a selection of fine and broad metal nibs.

Brushes

Before you discover the kinds of brushes most suited to your needs, you will most likely need to experiment with different types of brush.

To produce a broad wash as a single statement, for instance, you will need to use a flat brush, a mop or a one-stroke brush. Larger brushes retain more colour so that a sheet of paper can be covered quickly and evenly. When out sketching, you will find that a medium-sized sable brush – No 6 or No 8 – will generally suffice for both washes and more detailed work. Chinese brushes are essentially calligraphy brushes, but you may like the sensitive line they produce.

Chinese brushes.

¹/4 inch Prolene

¹/4 inch Sable/ Synthetic

1 inch Sable/ Synthetic

One-stroke brushes and a domed flat wash brush for broad washes.

Prolene Series 51

A broad wash brush designed for covering large areas with watercolour.

Round brushes for broad strokes and washes.

Dalon 66

Prolene 14

Series 7 sable brushes.

Series 16 sable brushes.

Prolene brushes

Holding Brushes

Just as a person's signature is highly personal, a painter will handle everything in terms of his own brushwork. You will sometimes hear artists and art critics talking about the 'handling' of a painting. This has to do with the individuality of the artist's touch. We recognize the difference between, say, a watercolour by Bonnington and one by Whistler by the difference in handling. The brush is an extension of the artist's eye – revealing the most tentative trace of the artist's own feelings.

In order to gain graphic control of the hand, the painter William Coldstream worked as an assistant sign-writer. The painting of letterforms is an excellent way of learning brush control.

For detailed work, the sable brush is usually cradled between the first and second fingers with pressure applied by the thumb. In my experience, the broader the brush, the farther down the handle it is held. Try holding the brush at the very tip of the handle, so that the smallest movement is amplified. Practice making strokes upwards and downwards, slowly and very rapidly, until you feel you have more control over the brush.

Controlling a fine sable brush. Notice how the brush is cradled for support between forefinger and thumb.

A broad one-stroke brush is used to lay a wash. It is held further down the handle to ensure greater control.

A Chinese brush is held at the top of the handle for a more fluid movement.

Practising line control with a No 4 sable brush.

A round brush is held loosely to produce a broad wash.

A backstroke with a mop produces a pale wash.

Maintaining Equipment

26

BRUSHES

Sable brushes are expensive and it should be an unbroken rule to clean them each time after use. The life of a sable brush will depend on the way it is used as well as how thoroughly it is cleaned. Try to keep brushes for different functions; a sable brush can take quite a lot of punishment, but try not to use it for any kind of scrubbing action. This will loosen hairs in the ferrule and spoil the shape of the brush.

TO CLEAN A BRUSH

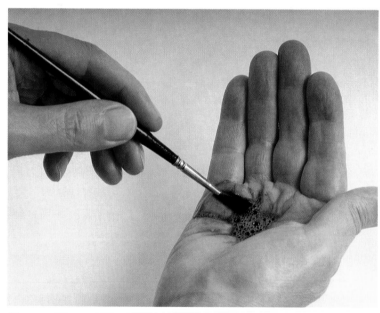

❶ *Pour a little detergent into the palm of your hand. Gently rotate the bristles to soak up the detergent.*

❷ *Rinse in warm water.*

PROTECTING YOUR BRUSHES

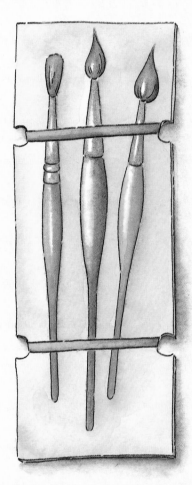

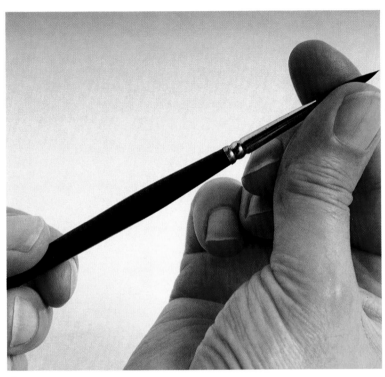

③ *Re-shape the bristles with your finger and thumb.*
Store brushes when not in use in a cylinder or on a protective backing card
(as illustrated right).

PAINTBOX AND PALETTE

Clean all mixing palettes after use and, more importantly, allow pans of watercolour to dry out before closing the box. This might prove difficult when you are travelling; if so, open the box when you return to your studio so that the colours can dry.

When using tubes of colour try to get into the habit of screwing the cap back on the tube *immediately* after use.

OTHER MATERIALS

A roll of kitchen paper always comes in useful whether you are working inside or out.

Keep two jars for mixing and rinsing colour and make sure they have screwtops that are watertight.

Good quality paint brushes are expensive to buy, but will give long service if looked after properly. One of the most common causes of damage is the inadequate protection of the brush hairs during transit. There are several ways to avoid this happening. Either retain the plastic cap which comes with the brush when purchased, or buy a specially designed rigid tube.

A very simple and inexpensive alternative is to make your own.

Cut a stout piece of cardboard taller than your largest brush. Cut four semi circular indents in the sides, as shown in the illustration above. Place two thick elastic bands

Washes

One of the main prerequisites for becoming a good water-colour painter is the ability to lay a good wash. By that, I mean being able to cover a relatively large sheet of paper with an evenly laid tone of diluted colour.

For the beginner, this is often the most daunting aspect of water-colour painting. There is no need for anxiety, however, providing that you take account of the following factors. Firstly, the quality and surface texture of the paper are important – whether it has too much size content or too little, whether it is too smooth or too coarse. Secondly, the angle of your sketchbook or drawing board and the angle of the brush to the paper can assist the flow of colour. Thirdly, the amount of colour loaded in your brush and the size of the brush in relation to the area to be covered makes a difference. Finally, the deftness and speed at which you work and (if you are working outside) the heat of the day, the wind or a damp atmosphere, affect the evaporation of colour. You can apply washes freely as Turner did, without precise bound-aries, or you can develop a blocking-in technique as Cotman did, by dividing the subject into simple shapes or blocks of colour. Freshness of colour is one of the main characteristics of water-colour, and this is lost to some extent if too many washes are superimposed on one another.

MIXING A WASH

Being a painter is sometimes like being a good cook – the mixing of the ingredients can greatly influence the finished result.

Though I would not personally worry about the kind of water used for producing a wash, there are some painters who believe that distilled water or even rain water will produce a better wash than hard water from a tap. There is some truth in this, since hard water has a tendency to curdle the paint.

Unless you find it too cumbersome, you should always have two jars of water – one for mixing colour, the other for rinsing your brushes. This will ensure cleaner results and you will need a change of water less often.

It is always better to mix more of a tint than you will actually need; the time taken to mix a fresh tint can spoil your concen-tration, and it will be difficult to match the first mixture exactly.

Try to ensure that the wash is free from lumps of undiluted pigment. Blend the colour thoroughly with your brush before you start, and also before you take up more colour on the brush.

STRETCHING PAPER

You will need a drawing board, or a similar firm support that is larger than the size of the watercolour paper. The paper is fixed to the board with gummed tape (gum-strip). This is coated on one side with a water-soluble gum which becomes tacky when moistened with a sponge.

First, immerse the paper completely in a bath filled with a few centimetres of cold water – a photographer's developing tray is ideal.

1 Allow the paper to soak so that there are no dry patches, then lift it out of the bath and drain off any excess water.

2 Next, place the paper centrally on your board and, with a finger, squeegee the edges so that they are just damp.

3 Cut the gum-strip into four lengths – longer than the four sides of the paper itself. Wet the tape with a damp sponge.

4 Press the tape firmly into position along each edge of the paper so that it covers an equal width of board and paper.

The paper should then be allowed to dry out – you can assist the drying after 15-20 minutes with a hair-dryer.

Watercolour papers of 300gsm / 140lb and heavier papers do not require stretching.

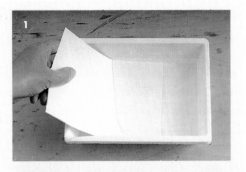

Laying Washes

LAYING A FLAT WASH

If you are laying a flat wash on dry paper, mix a sufficient quantity of paint in your mixing tray and fully load the brush. Tilt your board or sketchbook towards you at a slight angle. Make your first stroke across the top of the paper. As the colour begins to collect at the bottom of the stroke, pick it up with your brush and continue in this way with successive strokes, allowing a slight overlap where they join. Work towards the bottom of your sheet of paper, or the area you wish to cover, and remove excess paint by squeezing out your brush and lifting the residue so that the wash is even in tone.

An alternative method is to dampen the surface of the paper first – this is particularly desirable on papers which are heavily sized. Having dampened the paper, make sure that the surface is matt and not too wet. Any excess water should be blotted off before laying the wash. Tilt the board and proceed as before. A flat wash laid onto damp paper is softer and more diffused than a wash on dry paper.

A flat wash made with a 1½ inch flat brush and Fabriano (ROUGH) paper.

WASHING-OUT

This is a way of reversing-out white shapes from previously laid washes of colour. When the wash is dry, take a fine sable brush dipped in clean water, and soften the colour where you wish to remove it. Blot off the colour carefully with tissue.

You may need to repeat this operation until the paper appears as a clean white shape.

GRADUATED WASHES

A graduated wash starts with the colour at full strength and then, by dilution, the tone becomes paler until it is just a trace darker than the paper itself. Again, as with a flat wash, you can work either on dry or damp paper.

1 Mix the full tint and with a broad brush make the first stroke horizontally across the top of the paper.

2 Then, pick up a little water on the brush and dilute each stroke.

3 Continue until you have achieved a satisfactory gradation of tone.

WARNINGS AND AXIOMS

● Never touch a wash once it has been laid until it is thoroughly dry.

● Never, if you can avoid it, lay more than three washes over one another. Watercolour tends to dry lighter than when first painted. This is particularly true of darker tones.

● Make tests on paper samples before you buy expensive papers.

● Change damping water often.

Wet-in-Wet

32

Delacroix said that, 'One always has to spoil a picture a little bit in order to finish it'. Wet-in-wet is one of those techniques which are unpredictable and difficult to control. If you are the kind of artist who enjoys risk-taking, however, then the uncertain outcome of allowing washes to merge into one another while wet will appeal to you.

When working wet-in-wet you can dampen the paper first, either by sponging the whole sheet, or local areas of the painting such as the background or the sky. While the paper is still damp, float one or more washes onto the surface. The pigment will immediately be absorbed as it spreads, coagulates and forms rivulets of varying intensity. You can assist the flow by tilting your drawing board upright so that the colours run down, blending randomly with one another. A degree of control can be exercised by systematically blotting off patches of colour with tissue or cotton wool. More colour can be added before the first washes have dried out completely.

All techniques serve one purpose – to enable you to convey the particular qualities of some phenomenon you have witnessed yourself. There is no particular virtue in using the wet-in-wet technique for its own sake. The application of this technique is best suited to strongly atmospheric images – a landscape emerging from early morning mist, a turbulent sky or a seascape are all examples that come to mind.

RIGHT *An exercise using a large brush to make loosely painted slabs of colour on a dampened sheet of paper.*

BELOW *A rapidly executed sketch painted directly from the subject. Washes have been applied wet-in-wet onto RIVES H.P. paper.*

LEFT AND RIGHT *Two studies of a hillside in Tuscany painted directly from observation early in the morning when the mist rises from the valley.*

BELOW *This water-colour of a Swiss landscape demonstrates how the wet-in-wet technique can be controlled to suggest space and atmosphere.*

ABOVE *A wet-in-wet portrait painted against the light (contre jour) in 10-15 minutes.*

Dry Brush

34

The dry brush technique is essentially a means of providing texture in watercolour painting. It is also a way of lending graphic expression to what might be an otherwise static painting. When painting a landscape scene, for instance, you may feel the need to suggest rhythm and movement – particularly with the rendering of crops, grassland, trees and foliage.

In order to gain confidence in using this technique, you should make a few mark-making trials on scrap paper. You will need a textured paper – rough or NOT (cold-pressed). The brush should be starved of water before lifting pigment from your palette. Hold the brush lightly and make rapid strokes across the paper in a kind of sweeping action. The combination of dry pigment and the textured surface of the paper will produce a broken, granular stroke, which makes a pleasing contrast to flat washes.

Try different colours and vary the amount of water used. You could also experiment with different kinds of brushes.

ABOVE *Threave Castle, Scotland. Dry brush strokes have been used mainly in the foreground for reeds and grasses.*

ABOVE *Poppy field. Strong directional strokes of dry colour evoke the wave-like quality of crops and grassland.*

LEFT *Four variations of the dry brush technique. Notice how the colour is more opaque, and how the texture influences the quality of the marks made. To avoid making the colour too muddy, use short sharp strokes.*

Thin broad washes are used for the distant poppy field.

Dry brush work is used on the figure.

Gum arabic is added to red to stop the colour 'sinking'.

Dry brush strokes used for the field add a strong rhythmic element to the painting.

Resist and Spatter

These techniques are useful mainly to extend the atmospheric and textural qualities of watercolour. In landscape painting particularly, we sometimes need to find ways of responding visually to the rich complexity of natural forms and the effects that climate can have on them.

Masking fluid and candle wax are both substances which are resistant to water. They are usually applied to the surface of the paper before any washes are laid. Masking fluid is a kind of liquid rubber which dries rapidly. It has a distinctive pale lemon colour, so it is very easy to see the marks you are making. It can be applied with a brush (preferably an old one since the fluid is difficult to clean off) or a dip pen with a broad nib.

LEFT TOP *This speckled texture is produced by using a wax candle as a resist.* LEFT MIDDLE *Masking fluid has been used in* rapid strokes to create this grass-like texture. LEFT BOTTOM *Tone created by spattering.* ABOVE *The bristles of an old toothbrush are loaded with colour and spattered onto a masked-out area of the painting.*

Additionally, it can be spattered with a hog's-hair brush. When you have completed your masking out, and the fluid has dried, apply a wash of colour over the area you wish to cover, and allow to dry. When thoroughly dry, peel off the masking fluid, which will now look like a rubbery skin, by burnishing gently with an index finger, taking care not to damage the surface of the paper. The drawing you have made will then appear as a white shape reversed-out of the watercolour wash.

Candle wax is more difficult to see, therefore the results tend to be more random. You can use the wax as a flat wedged shape, or it can be sharpened to a point.

Spatter enhances the granular quality of the painting. You can either use a toothbrush or a hog's-hair brush. Load paint on plentifully and drag the bristles against the blunt edge of a knife or wire mesh. Areas of the painting can be masked off with scraps of paper where you don't want spatter to appear.

*Façade of church
stopped-out with masking fluid.*

*A country church in Norfolk.
This watercolour was painted on
site in late summer when colours
and tones become more muted.
The wax resist was used after a
preliminary drawing had been
made in pencil.*

*Wax resist used on
hedges and field.*

*Masking fluid used before
applying a wash of
Burnt Umber.*

Brush Drawing

When you are painting from direct observation you will generally be too absorbed in your subject to think very much about the kind of brush you are using or the kind of marks that it makes. In order to extend your range of mark-making, you should try a number of exercises which allow you to concentrate on the quality of image produced by using different types of brush. Try, for instance, making broad strokes of colour with a Hake 3 inch and, when dry, overlay a series of loose calligraphic squiggles with a No. 6 sable. Also try using brushes that are not normally associated with watercolour – such as a hog's-hair brush with a flat or round tip. This will produce very brittle strokes of colour. Chinese brushes, too, make a characteristic mark which is very different to that made with a sable. By extending your mark-making vocabulary in this way, you will feel more confident in dealing with most subjects. You will also be able to produce watercolours which are richer in terms of texture and contrast.

Exercises using different types of brush. Notice the effect of overlaying fine brushstrokes onto those made with broader bristles. The main purpose of carrying out this kind of exercise is that you will gain confidence in making lucid brushstrokes without feeling in anyway intimidated by the medium.

Brushstrokes made with Sable, Ox-hair, Hog's-hair and Chinese brushes.

Brush Drawing • *Basic Exercises*

This is the purest form of watercolour painting. To draw directly with a brush can be an immensely satisfying form of graphic expression. Drawings made with a brush and watercolour are often less self-conscious than those made with pen or pencil. This has something to do with the fact that the softness of the image lends a fluency to the drawing which is difficult to obtain in any other medium.

Almost any mark you make with a brush is a statement about form and shape as well as about colour and tone. Most importantly, you should first discover what kind of marks can be made with different types of brush. Try to work in terms of the medium, rather than trying to conceal the unique character of brushmarks by overworking the drawing.

LEFT *A portrait study made with a No. 5 sable brush. The underlying drawing has been made from direct observation using a pale wash of Alizarin Crimson and Lamp Black. When dry, other washes have been rapidly overlaid wet-in-wet.*

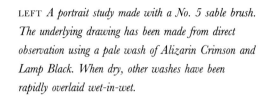

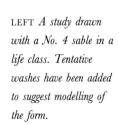

LEFT *A study drawn with a No. 4 sable in a life class. Tentative washes have been added to suggest modelling of the form.*

ABOVE *A direct study of an olive tree made as a notation for future reference. This sketch was completed in 10 minutes using a No. 8 sable brush.*

Pencil and Wash

LEFT *This page from a Venetian sketchbook shows the right kind of balance between pencil and colour.*

RIGHT *Another sketchbook page on which drawn pencil marks and colour work well together.*

The earliest watercolours were really tinted drawings – washes of pale colour were laid over pencil studies as a kind of embellishment to heighten the drawing.

Quite often the tinted drawings were preliminary studies for engravings. A number of early English watercolourists, Turner and Cotman included, were employed to add watercolour to ready-made prints.

Line and wash – the classic watercolour technique – came into its own when wealthy 18th-century patrons commissioned picturesque studies of scenery along the 'Grand Tour' of Europe.

John Cozens (1752-97) was one of the first watercolourists to use line and wash to depict the Italian landscape. By the beginning of the 19th century, watercolour painting was considered to be an art in its own right. Turner, much influenced by Cozens, travelled to the Continent in 1802 as far as the Swiss Alps. There followed a series of watercolour paintings recording a journey down the Rhine and in 1819, at the age of forty-four, Turner

visited Italy for the first time and produced some of his finest watercolours. The tradition of classic watercolour established by the early English watercolourists has continued to the present day – alongside computer-aided photography and video-recorders! My own view is that you cannot truly know a place until you have drawn it. When I sit before a scene trying to register line for line, tone for tone, I gain an understanding of the subject which is indelibly stored in my memory.

For pencil and wash I prefer to use a paper made from 100% cotton – Saunders or Fabriano are ideal. The soft surface of these papers is very receptive to both pencil and watercolour. A paper that is too heavily textured tends to break up the pencil marks; too smooth a paper produces unsatisfactory washes.

The balance between line and wash is critical – there is no point in simply filling-in a previously drawn pencil outline with washes. The pencil drawing might provide an underlying structure but it is also an integral part of the whole painting.

I find a medium-soft pencil, such as 2B or 3B, ideal to produce the right tonal balance between line and wash.

Perhaps the most difficult aspect of this technique for the beginner is to learn how to be selective. When you start to draw, you need to be conscious of the fact that the drawing is only a part of the total image – you must allow for the fact that subsequent washes of colour will work alongside the pencil drawing, rather than displace or colour it. In other words, both line and wash should be used descriptively to produce a single image without any separation of technique.

ABOVE *The city of Segovia drawn from a distance in pale pencil tones with delicate washes that do not cancel out the drawing.*

RIGHT *A tentative use of the pencil in this painting allows coloured washes to work independently.*

Pen and Wash

44

Pen and ink when used with washes of watercolour can work particularly well in paintings which rely on closely-related tones. The drawing pen produces strong linear marks which provide an interesting contrast to flat washes of colour.

The 17th-century painter, Claude Lorraine (1600-82), produced pen and wash drawings of great lucidity, using washes of Bistre, Sepia and Indigo. This strongly monochromatic form of line and wash painting also found favour with the English painter, Samuel Palmer (1805-81). Palmer's visionary paintings of Shoreham are charged with symbolism.

The traditional dip pen can be useful when used with a variety of nibs – the finest of which are known as mapping pens. Broader drawing nibs are usually quite springy and are flexible enough to suit most subjects.

Reed and quill pens, which historically preceded the metal nib, produce a wonderful irregular line which is less mechanical than the conventional dip pen.

You can make your own pens with short sticks of bamboo of different diameters. With a sharp knife, trim off about 4cm/1½ inches at an acute angle until you have a sharp point. If you cut half a dozen pens, you can vary the tip of the pen from a fine point to a broad chisel shape. You will find that the spongy texture of the hollowed inside of the bamboo retains the ink sufficiently to be able to draw freely. Old fountain pens can sometimes produce an interesting quality of line, particularly if the nib is worn.

Felt and plastic-tipped pens are convenient to use, although the uniformity of line that they produce can be restricting. If you do

A landscape in Italy. Washes were applied after the pen drawing was completed. Care must be taken not to cancel out the sense of light created by the broken line of the pen drawing.

not want your drawn lines to 'bleed', you should use a water-proof ink. On the other hand, you may happen to like the way that non-waterproof ink will dissolve when watercolour is brushed over the surface. As well as black ink, there is a good range of coloured inks which are shellac-based and waterproof.

To gain experience of working with pen and wash, and to control tones, you could produce a Sepia pen drawing with over-laid washes graduating from Ochre to Burnt Umber on a toned paper. Try also a simple exercise in mark-making with different types of pen. It is important that you are able to work at ease with your materials – especially since mistakes in pen and ink are difficult to rectify. Finally, always try to work in terms of the medium – a good pen and wash drawing should bear the imprint of the materials used, and not look like something else.

ABOVE LEFT
A portrait drawing made with a fountain pen using non-waterproof ink which has dissolved slightly after a wash of watercolur was overlaid.

LEFT *A strong drawing made with a reed pen. A single wash of Cadmium Orange is used effectively.*

Layering Techniques

When two or three transparent washes are laid one over the other, there are unexpected changes of colour and tone. This, in essence, is the main characteristic of the medium – that colour and tone accrue gradually, rather than being put down at full strength as they are in oil painting, for example.

Traditionally, the watercolourist works from light to dark – in landscape this usually means starting with the palest tones in the sky then going on to the middle-tones of the middle-distance and the stronger tones of the foreground. If you look at a watercolour by Cézanne, however, you will discover that the forms are made-

up of tiny vibrant patches of layered colour. Moreover, each colour is made to work throughout the whole painting and is not confined to a specific area.

If, for instance, you are painting a landscape view, the pale tone you have used for the sky might also provide an undertone for hills, grass, shadows and so on. Similarly, other forms in the landscape, such as the foliage on trees, might need to be built up in closely-related layers of colour, rather than as a single wash.

Knowing precisely how colour and tonal values can be established can only come from practice and experience.

The dense foliage is built up in layers of colour from pale blue to olive green.

The pale wash of Cobalt Blue used for the sky also underpins the foliage of the trees and grass.

A pale wash of green is overlaid with Terre Verte.

ABOVE *A Tuscan landscape using layered colour.*

LEFT *An exercise using layered washes of the same hue.*

ABOVE *An exercise in layering washes at different strengths – notice the tonal variation.*

LEFT *A Tuscan land-scape which employs both layered colour and wet-in-wet colour. The silvery-grey of the olive trees is achieved by adding a little white body colour. Tonal unity is maintained by restricting the number of colours used.*

Colour

48

ir Isaac Newton (1642-1727) was able to demonstrate that, although sunlight, or white light, is 'uncoloured', it is made up of seven coloured rays: violet, indigo, blue, green, yellow, orange and red. We see colour in objects that reflect and absorb these rays to a greater or lesser degree. An object which reflected the rays completely would be white or uncoloured. If that same object absorbed the same rays, it would look black.

The artist working in watercolour must consider colour in an entirely different way to the artist working in oils, acrylic or gouache. The full colour value of a watercolour painting accrues as one transparent film of pigment is laid over another. This demands a certain amount of premeditation on the part of the artist inasmuch as he or she must be aware of the effect that one or more colours will have when combined to produce a particular hue. One needs to be aware of the way that different colour combinations can produce the colours required for the subject being painted. If, for instance, one were painting a Mediterranean landscape, the darker olive greens might be mixed from Lamp Black, Gamboge Yellow and Burnt Umber. The silvery colour of the leaves of an olive tree, on the other hand, might be mixed from a combination of Viridian, Naples Yellow and a little white body colour. You will obviously need to experiment with washes to discover for yourself exactly how to achieve the colours you are searching for.

Colours can basically be mixed in four ways. They may be fused together in equal quantities thus creating a new colour. A slight trace of one colour can be used to diffuse or moderate a stronger colour. A third colour might serve to break the colour resulting from an equal mixing of the first two. Opaque shades and tints are created by adding black or white with either pure or previously mixed colour.

Remember that every colour in your paintbox represents a tone as well as a colour – if the colour is applied with a brush starved of water it can appear as opaque as gouache or, conversely, when greatly diluted, as a pale tint that is only a fraction darker in tone than the paper itself.

We see colour in nature as a harmony of contrasts – light against dark, one complementing another, cool against warm. At the same time every object has its own, unique colour. The specific or 'local' colour of a tiled roof might be a terracotta red but, like all colours, it is modified by light. The appearance of colour is dependent on how and where it is placed – the English painter Walter Sickert (1860-1942) used to say that, 'the colour in the shadows must be the sister of the colour in the light.' Everything is relative; the brilliance and intensity of a fishing trawler painted red would be considerably enhanced by the surrounding drab colour of the harbour walls.

The artist can only hope to produce an approximation of the colours he sees in nature – the best watercolourists work in terms of suggestion rather than overstatement. The watercolours of Cozens, Cotman, Turner and Cézanne look effortless – as if they have captured a moment in time, rather than being the product of prolonged study. There is a certain 'hit or miss' element in watercolour painting which sometimes means that for every painting you produce which is reasonably satisfactory, there will perhaps be three or four that might have to be abandoned. Unlike oil painting or acrylic, watercolours rarely benefit from being re-worked.

The best way of improving your understanding of colour is to work as often as possible from direct observation – matching the colours you see to the pigments in your paintbox. In cultivating this habit, you will begin to remember how certain colours and tones are achieved and, in time, you will be able to look at colours in the landscape and know in your own mind exactly how you would mix such colours.

An irregular colour wheel which heightens awareness of the transparent nature of the medium.

A useful exercise in creating colour by overlaying two or three patches of different colours in varying tones. Notice particularly the effect of laying pale, dilute washes over more solid colours.

Tone

RIGHT *A landscape in Tuscany. A wash of Venetian Red is applied freely using a large brush on Saunders HP paper.*

LEFT *The main forms of the landscape are painted in with Umber using a No. 6 sable brush.*

RIGHT *Greater tonal definition is given to the painting by adding darker washes and a little body colour in the foreground.*

RIGHT *Graduations of colour painted as a tonal scale – this simple exercise can help to increase* *your understanding of the enormous tonal variations that can be produced with watercolour.*

The way that areas of light and dark are distributed in your painting is as important to the overall design as the placing of objects in your composition. One of the main reasons why the watercolours produced by beginners sometimes fail is that they lack tonal unity.

It is surprising how often poor colour values in a painting are due to not giving sufficient consideration to tonal relationships. In order to understand how tones can work in your painting, you should first try to forget the convention of describing forms by defining them with a drawn outline. Get into the habit of seeing things in terms of degrees of tone – light, medium and dark.

You could try, for instance, to produce a watercolour painting in which you forget all about local colour and restrict yourself to using three related tones. Additionally, you could work on a tinted paper – buff-coloured for warm tones, grey for cool tones. Watercolour tones depend on the amount of pigment you use. Light tones are produced by adding a trace of pigment to a lot of water, dark tones with just enough water on your brush to soften the pigment. The sense of depth and recession in landscape, is recreated in painting by the intervals between light and dark tones – the tones further away from the eye are lighter than those in the middle-distance, and become progressively darker towards the foreground.

Individual hues all have their own tones. The three brightest primary colours, for example, would register as follows on a 0 – 10 scale: yellow 4, red 6 and blue 7.

When you are painting a landscape view, look at the scene before you through half-closed eyes. This results in a kind of diffused blurring of detail, which enables you to judge tonal values in a more unified way.

In the best tonal paintings, detail is sacrificed in order to give more emphasis to the design of the painting. In landscape, tonal harmonies are usually found at first light and towards dusk, when conspicuous detail is lost in shadow and forms are softly revealed.

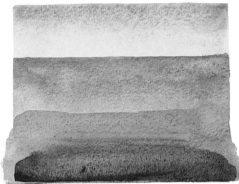

A basic tonal exercise which demonstrates how closely related colours and tones can be used to suggest depth and recession.

A view of the Italian hilltown, Monterrigioni. Compare the tonal unity in the original painting with that in a black and white photograph of the painting.

Composition

66

*To put together to for a whole esp.
artistically; order, arramge*

99

This simple definition from the Oxford Dictionary is as good as any – composition has to do with the conscious ordering of the various elements of a painting into a harmonious whole. Delacroix (1798-1863) said that, 'one line alone has no meaning; a second one is needed to give it expression.'

The process of composing begins from the moment you select a particular viewpoint, before you have made any marks on the paper. Objects in nature are never isolated – they are relative. Though a single feature might command your attention – a solitary church on a hillside, for instance – it is seen in relation to the broader view of surrounding hills and sky, roads, trees and footpaths. If it was your intention to convey this sense of isolation in your watercolour painting, then scale would be critical, and you would paint the church from a greater distance. If, on the other hand, you were more interested in saying something about the architectural detail of the same church, then you would have to move much closer to your subject. Composition, in this sense, is determined by your intentions.

Landscape is without a doubt the most popular subject for watercolourists, yet it is potentially the most difficult to handle in terms of composition. Landscape is indeterminate and orderless – you need to have a strong sense of design to be able to visually harness all the random elements which are positioned at different levels and recede into the distance. One advantage that you have over the photographer is that you can simply leave out any detail which you feel might spoil the balance of your composition. The composition of seascapes is very much dependent on where the line of horizon is placed. Supposing, for example, you wanted to make a dramatic stormy sky the main feature of your painting, then you would place the horizon line low in your composition in order to provide the right emphasis. Conversely, if you were painting a 'Turneresque' sea study, then the horizon

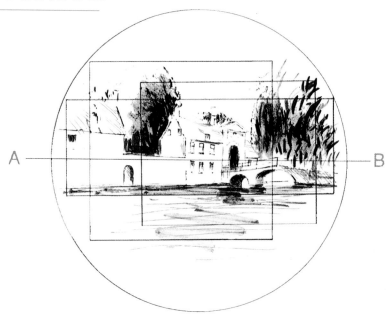

*This diagram represents the circle of vision.
The different rectangles suggest the choices available in terms of composition.*

line would either be high in your composition or would disappear altogether.

Classical painters, such as Poussin (1594-1665), often used pictorial devices to lead the eye towards the most important part of their composition. Paths, lines of trees, rivers and bridges were carefully positioned to draw the eye towards the group of figures which were the focal point of the composition.

The 'acid-test' of a well-composed painting, however, is that the viewer should be unaware that the artist has imposed any kind of pre-determined plan on his work. A painting in which the composition is too self-conscious will distract attention from the subject itself. The artist needs to be something of a tightrope walker and a dancer – the basic framework of the composition supporting the free expression of the brushwork.

When painting a still life subject you will find that you have much greater control over the composition since the objects you are painting can be arranged at will. We know that Cézanne used to spend hours arranging his still life groups – changing folds in cloth, moving bottles, jugs and bowls of fruit until he felt instinctively the relationship to be right. This sense of 'rightness' in composition is not something that can be taught; it comes with observation and experience.

There are, however, certain established ground rules in composition which you might find helpful. The best known device for dividing space aesthetically is known as the 'Golden Section'. To give you some idea how this works, try the following simple experiment. Take a sheet of A4 writing paper and fold it in half three times in succession. When you open the paper flat again you will notice that it is divided into eight equal parts. Draw a line with a pen on the fifth fold – this is the Golden Section on a 3:5 ratio

(alternative ratios might be 2:3, 5:8, or 8:13). This device works best in those compositions where there is a significant vertical element – a figure or even a tree or lamppost, which provides a kind of axis for the whole painting.

The process of composing a painting can continue even after it is finished. Try, for instance, placing a square window mount over a landscape-shaped painting in your sketchbook. You will discover that as you move the mount slightly you can isolate parts of your painting in such a way that it looks entirely different – and perhaps even better!

A simple viewing device cut from black card will help you initially to isolate the main areas of interest in your composition.

Perspective

All lines which are in fact parallel appear to meet at a point on the horizon we call the vanishing point.

Perspective is really a kind of visual trick – it is the means by which we create the illusion of three dimensions.

We see things in depth – that is to say, we see objects disposed at varying distances from each other and from ourselves. When we draw 'in perspective', we are trying to represent what we have seen in three dimensions on a flat sheet of two-dimensional paper. It is perfectly possible to do this by simply trying to register what you see without being conscious of the laws of perspective. On the other hand, a basic understanding of these laws will enable you to draw complex subjects, such as townscapes, with more confidence.

The principle of perspective is that objects which are of the same size appear to diminish in size as they get farther away from the eye of the beholder.

When we say that a drawing is 'out of perspective', we usually mean that certain lines have been drawn to the wrong angle. From where I am sitting as I write, I am looking through a window over the rooftops of the town towards the sea. If I were to trace the outline of this directly onto the window glass, it would become apparent how the roofs of buildings, which are of a similar size, are reduced in size towards the horizon.

THE EYE-LEVEL

Eye-level is the term used to express the height of the artist's eye from the ground – assuming that the lines are parallel to the ground and that the ground is flat. Lines which are above your eye-level are drawn down to the horizon or eye-level. Conversely, lines below are drawn up towards the eye-level. If you stand up or sit down, the eye-level moves up and down too.

Try this simple experiment. Stand in a large room and hold your pencil horizontally at arm's length. Look at the lines above your eye-level – the ceiling, for instance. Notice how the lines slope and try to judge the angle against the line of your pencil. If you then try to draw on a sheet of paper what you have seen – you are drawing in perspective.

THE PICTURE PLANE

The picture plane is an imaginary transparent vertical screen between you and the subject. It is set at the distance from the artist where the drawing or painting is intended to begin.

When, for example, you think of buildings being parallel to your painting, they would also be parallel to the picture plane.

There are no straight lines in nature and one should not apply the rules of perspective too self-consciously. Lines of construction are useful inasmuch as they contribute to the success of the finished work. Accuracy in drawing, however, has more to do with searching observation than with mere technical proficiency.

Three studies of the Stansted Airport Terminal designed by Sir Norman Foster. The basic shapes of contemporary architecture in a particular setting often demonstrate the principles of perspective very clearly.

THE
PROJECTS

How the Projects Work

The first part of this book has dealt with the essential techniques of watercolour painting. Learning how to handle techniques and understanding the particular characteristics of the medium is, of course, terribly important. Just as the novice pianist must necessarily practise the scales and learn chords, so the artist must be able to use a medium with fluency. Nothing, however, should deter the artist from starting to work from observation as soon as possible and to do this you must be able to use techniques expressly to say what you have to say about a particular subject. If you concentrate too much on technique, you will never arrive at precision – if you concentrate on precision, you will arrive at technique.

Many artists using watercolours for the first time are fearful of making mistakes, but the greatest mistake you can make in life is to be continuously feeling you will make one! Almost all our faults are more pardonable than the methods we resort to to hide them. In the Project Section which follows you will see how three artists have approached the same subjects in terms of their own personal vision and technique.

IAN POTTS is prepared to take risks – pushing the medium around until he arrives at a particular balance of colour, tone and linear description. His watercolours bear the imprint of someone who is more concerned with trying to respond to something seen momentarily, than slavishly trying to follow some pre-orientated plan. His unique technique of first applying colour with crumpled tissue, blotting areas off, and re-stating forms, allows greater freedom. There are, of course, times when the paintings may become overworked or don't dry in quite the way he had wanted, but he is essentially exploiting watercolour in its purest form – registering exquisite qualities of light in the process.

ANTHONY COLBERT handles the medium with a maturity that is very evident in paintings such as his Tuscany landscape (pages 134 and 135). He believes in doing preliminary drawings to gain a closer understanding of the subject and to provide an underlying structure to the painting. He gives careful consideration to the composition of his paintings – an aspect of painting that is all too often neglected by contemporary artists.

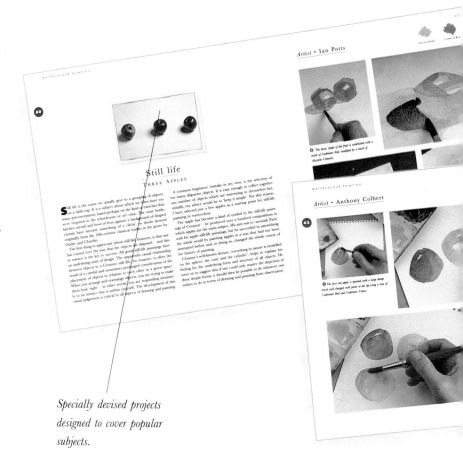

Specially devised projects designed to cover popular subjects.

DEBORAH JAMESON uses the classic watercolour technique of line and wash. The preliminary drawings made in pencil are not simply filled in with colour – she is able to produce the right balance between line and wash, so that they work together.

At the end of each project there is a critique which offers a brief appraisal of the work done. You may find yourself disagreeing with some of the comments made or you might have some criticisms of your own. You might even feel that you could produce something better. If so, I will leave you with the following thought from Goethe: 'We should talk less and draw more. Personally , I would like to renounce speech altogether and, like organic nature, communicate everything I have to say in sketches.'

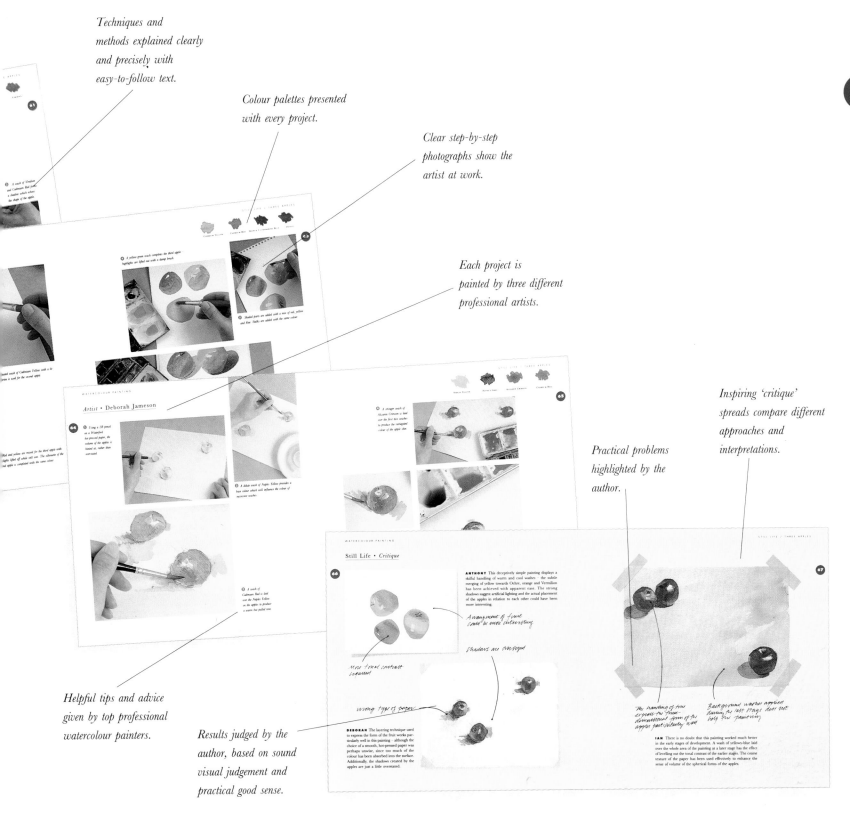

Techniques and methods explained clearly and precisely with easy-to-follow text.

Colour palettes presented with every project.

Clear step-by-step photographs show the artist at work.

Each project is painted by three different professional artists.

Inspiring 'critique' spreads compare different approaches and interpretations.

Practical problems highlighted by the author.

Helpful tips and advice given by top professional watercolour painters.

Results judged by the author, based on sound visual judgement and practical good sense.

Still life

THREE APPLES

Still life is the name we usually give to a grouping of objects on a table-top. It is a subject about which we often have too many preconceptions; based perhaps on the kind of exercises that were required in the schoolroom or art class. The wine bottle, kitchen utensil and bowl of fruit against a background of draped curtain have become something of a cliché, no doubt derived originally from the 18th-century classical studies in the genre by Oudry and Chardin.

The first thing to appreciate about still life, however, is that one has control over the way that the objects are disposed – and this in essence is the key to success. All good still-life paintings have an underlying unity of design. The apparently casual relationship between objects in a Cézanne still life, for instance, is often the result of a careful and sometimes prolonged consideration of the placement of objects in relation to each other in a given space. When you arrange and rearrange objects, you are trying to make them look 'right' – in other words, you are responding intuitively to an instinct that is within yourself. The development of this visual judgement is critical to all aspects of drawing and painting.

A common beginners' mistake in my view, is the selection of too many disparate objects. It is easy enough to collect together any number of objects which are interesting in themselves but, initially, my advice would be to 'keep it simple'. For this reason, I have selected just a few apples as a starting point for still-life painting in watercolour.

The apple has become a kind of symbol in the still-life paintings of Cézanne – he produced over a hundred compositions in which apples are the main subject. His aim was to 'astonish Paris' with his apple still-life paintings, but he succeeded in astonishing the whole world by painting apples in a way that had not been attempted before and, in doing so, changed the whole course of the history of painting.

Cézanne's well-known dictum, 'everything in nature is modelled on the sphere, the cone and the cylinder', helps to explain his feeling for the underlying form and structure of all objects. He went on to suggest that if one could only master the depiction of these simple forms, it should then be possible to do whatever one wishes to do in terms of drawing and painting from observation.

Artist • Ian Potts

YELLOW OCHRE   CADMIUM RED   ALIZARIN CRIMSON   VIRIDIAN

1 *The basic shape of the fruit is established with a wash of Cadmium Red, modified by a touch of Alizarin Crimson.*

2 *A wash of Viridian and Cadmium Red forms a shadow which echoes the shape of the apple.*

3 *The modelling of the fruit is developed in terms of colour and tone by applying successive layered washes.*

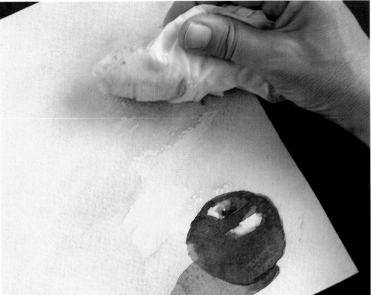

4 *A pale blue-green wash mixed from Viridian and Yellow Ochre is laid over the whole sheet of paper — excepting the highlights on the apples.*

Artist • Anthony Colbert

1 *The first red apple is painted with a large damp brush well-charged with paint at the tip using a mix of Cadmium Red and Cadmium Yellow.*

2 *A graduated wash of Cadmium Yellow with a little Ultramarine is used for the second apple.*

3 *Red and yellow are mixed for the third apple with highlights lifted off while still wet. The silhouette of the second apple is completed with the same colour.*

CADMIUM YELLOW

CADMIUM RED

FRENCH ULTRAMARINE BLUE

INDIGO

63

4 *A yellow-green wash completes the third apple –*
highlights are lifted out with a damp brush.

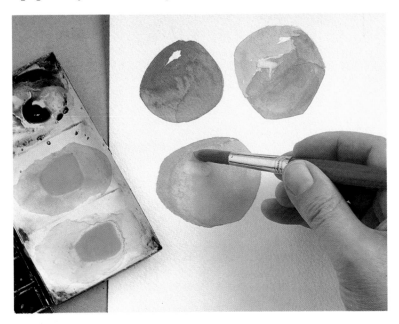

5 *Shaded parts are added with a mix of red, yellow*
and blue. Stalks are added with the same colour.

6 *Cast shadows are*
produced with a wash
of Indigo.

Artist • Deborah Jameson

64

❶ *Using a 2B pencil on a Waterford hot-pressed paper, the volume of the apples is hinted at, rather than overstated.*

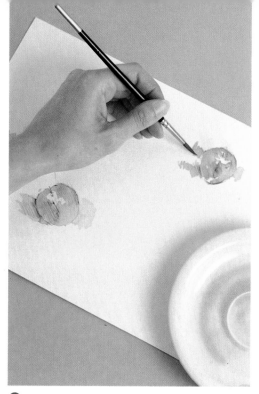

❷ *A dilute wash of Naples Yellow provides a base colour which will influence the colour of successive washes.*

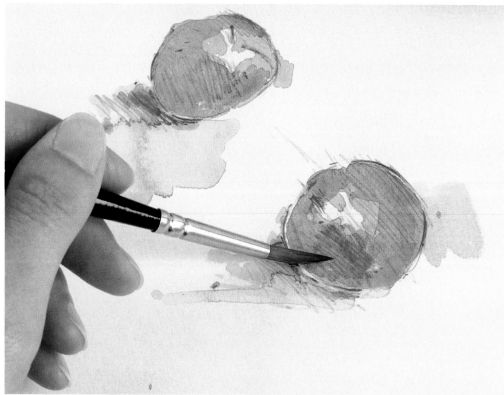

❸ *A wash of Cadmium Red is laid over the Naples Yellow on the apples to produce a warm but pallid tone.*

NAPLES YELLOW   PAYNE'S GREY   ALIZARIN CRIMSON   CADMIUM RED

65

4 *A stronger wash of Alizarin Crimson is laid over the first two washes to produce the variegated colour of the apple skin.*

5 *This detail shows how the same Alizarin Crimson is extended to the shadow as a base colour for the darker tone to be added at the final stage.*

6 *A final wash of Payne's Grey is used to lend expression to the modelling of the forms in terms of light and shadow.*

Still Life • *Critique*

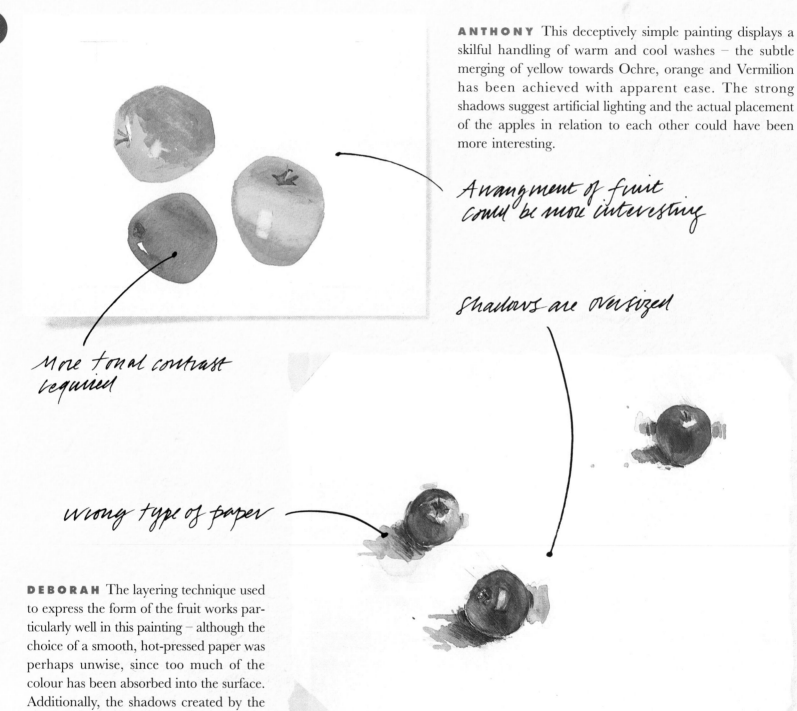

ANTHONY This deceptively simple painting displays a skilful handling of warm and cool washes – the subtle merging of yellow towards Ochre, orange and Vermilion has been achieved with apparent ease. The strong shadows suggest artificial lighting and the actual placement of the apples in relation to each other could have been more interesting.

Arrangement of fruit could be more interesting

Shadows are oversized

More tonal contrast required

wrong type of paper

DEBORAH The layering technique used to express the form of the fruit works particularly well in this painting – although the choice of a smooth, hot-pressed paper was perhaps unwise, since too much of the colour has been absorbed into the surface. Additionally, the shadows created by the apples are just a little overstated.

The handing of tone
express the three-
dimensional form of the
apples particularly well

Background washes applied
during the last stage does not
help the painting

IAN There is no doubt that this painting worked much better
in the early stages of development. A wash of yellowy-blue laid
over the whole area of the painting at a later stage has the effect
of levelling out the tonal contrast of the earlier stages. The coarse
texture of the paper has been used effectively to enhance the
sense of volume of the spherical forms of the apples.

Light and Shadow

ANTIQUE HEAD

We tend to see most things in terms of contrasts, which can be strong and sharply defined or more subtle and barely perceived. Additionally, with a graduated scale of tone from light to dark, we also need to perceive colour which is modulated in warm or cool hues. Colour and tone need to be harnessed together to produce a satisfactory painting. When working in watercolour, it is fairly easy to produce bold washes of primary colour, but to produce a more subtle range of tone requires much more control.

For this project, a white cast of an antique head is seen against a white background. The aim of this project is twofold – to gain experience of controlling pale washes of colour to render the subtle tones of light and shade and to learn to mix a wider range of warm and cool tints without adding body colour (gouache).

From a basic set of watercolours, you will be surprised just how many shades of grey you can mix. Traces of Umber, Ochre and Cadmium Red produce warm tints; the blues – Cerulean, Cobalt and Monastral with a hint of Lamp Black – produce cooler tints. It would be a useful background exercise to make your own chart of warm and cool tints – perhaps 20 of each with notes to remind you of the colour combinations used in mixing each tint.

In a painting of this kind, the white surface of the paper itself plays an important part, as does the quality of light falling on the antique head. Because the head is cast in white, and the background is also white, the local colour is neither warm nor cool. If, however, the light is a cold light, the resulting shadows will tend to be warm. Conversely, if the light source is warm then the shadows will be cool.

All of this may seem confusing at first but, with practice, you will begin to understand how colour as colour and light as light are combined in the adumbrated washes used to build up a painting. The more you paint from direct observation, the more you will begin to see shades of tone and hues of colour which previously would have gone unnoticed.

Artist • Ian Potts

PAYNE'S GREY

HOOKER'S GREEN

VIRIDIAN

INDIGO

COBALTL

1 *The artist uses an unstretched sheet of Bockingford (NOT) 300gsm / 140lb paper. The surface of the paper is dampened slightly and a background wash of Viridian mixed with a little Hooker's Green is laid in a controlled movement with tissue. The wash follows the contours of the head. When dry, a stronger wash of the same colour begins to define the features of the head and areas of shadow. Further adjustments are made by dabbing off some of the washes with a paper towel.*

2 *The modelling of the form continues with a No.8 sable loaded with a mix of Indigo and a touch of Payne's Grey to produce a darker hue.*

3 *(Detail) The paper is re-dampened and further washes are laid and lifted, in successive layers, until the balance of tone seems to be about right. The folds in the hair are dealt with at this stage, to suggest a sculptured low-relief.*

4 *An inky blue-black wash provides the darkest tone in the painting and intensifies the contrast even further.*

5 *Certain passages of the painting are blotted off with a paper towel while the colour is still wet.*

Artist • Anthony Colbert

70

1 *A wash of pale Indigo is laid as a base colour for the painting, using a Hake 3 inch, and allowed to dry. The wash is then repeated over the background, isolating the shape of the antique head.*

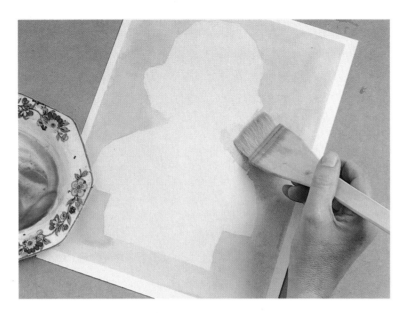

2 *Pale shades are blocked in using the same colour loaded onto a No. 8 sable brush.*

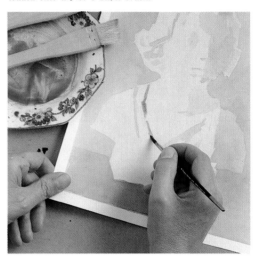

3 *The area of the cast shadow is dampened and a stronger mix of Indigo with a little Alizarin Crimson is brushed in.*

NAPLES YELLOW ALIZARIN CRIMSON INDIGO

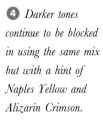

4 *Darker tones continue to be blocked in using the same mix but with a hint of Naples Yellow and Alizarin Crimson.*

6 *The tonal modulation is completed with a final dark wash of Indigo.*

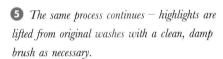

5 *The same process continues – highlights are lifted from original washes with a clean, damp brush as necessary.*

Artist • Deborah Jameson

72

1 *A Saunders hot-pressed paper has been selected for this project. The basic proportions of the antique cast are tentatively stated with a soft pencil.*

2 *The drawing is further developed to establish tonal values.*

3 *A much-diluted wash of Naples Yellow serves to heighten the contrast as it is laid over the drawing.*

NAPLES YELLOW   PAYNE'S GREY   LAMP BLACK

4 *The folds of the form are picked up in Naples Yellow.*

5 *A granular wash of Lamp Black follows the form of the head and provides further contrast.*

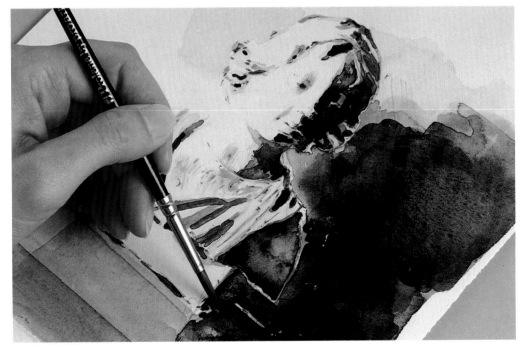

6 *The darkest tones are produced by overlaying a wash of Payne's Grey which also adds a hint of blue to the areas of shadow.*

Light and Shadow • *Critique*

Overall colour too blue

IAN This painting demonstrates just how much can be achieved with a few carefully co-ordinated washes which are closely related in tone and colour.

The artist has resisted the temptation to overwork the painting by the addition of too much sharply-defined detail. As in all the best watercolours, the painting retains the sense of suspended fluidity.

The colour is perhaps a little too blue – a more restrained grey-blue wash might have worked better.

DEBORAH The colour in this painting is of a warmer hue than the others - though, in the final stage, a near blue-black balances the warmth of the Naples Yellow. The artist has made good use of the white surface of the hot-pressed paper as an integral part of the image. My own feeling, however, is that it worked best at the second stage of development, when only a single wash of Naples Yellow had been added to the pencil drawing.

final stage overworked

ANTHONY This painting makes good use of soft and hard washes to create the illusion of a three-dimensional sculptural form.

It is clear that a considerable amount of premeditation on the part of the artist has been necessary to establish how best to employ washes with economy while at the same time suggesting modelling and graduation of tone from light to shadow. Again, it is perhaps too blue – and the white surface of the paper might have been used to better advantage.

Portrait

GIRL READING

The experience gained from the first two projects can now be used to advantage in painting a portrait. Watercolour is a most suitable medium for portrait painting, since the best portraits are usually those which employ a few colours and closely related tones – paintings by Rembrandt (1606-69), for instance, are almost entirely monochromatic, relying as they do on dramatic tonal contrast. Bright, primary colours tend to distract and dilute the tonal unity that necessarily directs our attention towards the expression of the person portrayed.

To talk of producing a 'likeness' of someone refers not just to external appearances, but also to the way that the particular expression and demeanour of the sitter can hint at character and personality. A good portrait must be more than mere imitative photo-realism – it should, by sheer force of statement, uncover the emotional state of the sitter. In this respect, a rapidly-executed

drawing or watercolour can sometimes be far more revealing than a prolonged study in oil painting.

Most people when sitting for a portrait will present a particular stance or gesture which betrays an aspect of their personality. The eyes, ears, nose and mouth are the primary organs of the senses and often provide a key to intrinsic character. The process of selection is all important – one needs to ask oneself, 'what are the essential features which are unique to the person who is sitting before me?' and, 'how can I best express those qualities, in terms of the medium I am using?'.

Before starting a portrait, therefore, one should consider different viewpoints – profile, full-face or three-quarter. Is the subject best seen from a high or low vantage point? Should one stand two or six metres distant? Consider also the lighting and try to keep the background simple and free from extraneous detail.

Artist • Ian Potts

YELLOW OCHRE

RAW UMBER

VANDYKE BROWN

COBALT BLUE

ALIZARIN CRIMSON

77

1 *Having first dampened the paper, the lightest tones of the painting are laid with tissues, wet-in-wet. When dry, the main form of the figure is blocked in with a wash of Cobalt Blue, which contrasts with the warmer tones of the background.*

Painting onto damp paper allows the features of the portrait to remain in soft focus.

2 *The darker tones of the hair are added with a wash mixed from Cobalt Blue and Vandyke Brown – producing a near black. The flesh tone is also heightened with a wash containing traces of Yellow Ochre and Raw Umber – the same colour as is overlaid in the background.*

3 *Using a No.6 sable brush, details such as the pattern on the scarf are established. Other details are tentatively suggested with a few strokes of the brush – avoiding overstatement.*

4 *(Detail) Notice how the edge of the face is defined by a single wash of colour.*

5 *Colour is lifted off with a paper towel.*

Artist • Anthony Colbert

78

1 *A light wash mixed from Yellow Ochre and Cadmium Red is laid over the whole area and allowed to dry. The main features of the portrait are lightly pencilled in.*

2 *An underpainting is established using washes of Burnt Sienna, Cadmium Red and Burnt Umber in varying strengths.*

3 *Some highlights are lifted out and other washes darkened to provide tonal balance.*

YELLOW OCHRE

CADMIUM RED

BURNT UMBER

RAW SIENNA

COBALT BLUE

INDIGO

79

4 *The bright primary colours of the scarf are painted in.*

5 *The hair and details on the face and hands are painted with Burnt Sienna. The same colour is used for the details of panelling behind the figure. A strong wash of Indigo is applied to the coat and scarf.*

6 *Using a No. 4 sable, fine details are added – the face is modelled with darker browns and flesh tints made from Yellow Ochre warmed with Cadmium Red. Cast shadows are produced with a mix of Burnt Umber and Indigo. In the hair, the light areas are painted with Burnt Sienna, the darker tones with Burnt Umber.*

A second wash is added to the coat and the wall is painted green to complement the warmer colours in the rest of the painting.

Artist • Deborah Jameson

80

❶ *Having selected a profile view of the model, a preliminary drawing registers the main features of the pose.*

❷ *A wash of Payne's Grey follows the contours of the profile and works as an underpainting for the washes to follow.*

❸ *Using a broader Chinese brush, a wash of Naples Yellow neutralises the Payne's Grey, and provides the first flesh tint.*

 NAPLES YELLOW

 PAYNE'S GREY

 VANDYKE BROWN

 ALIZARIN CRIMSON

 BURNT SIENNA

4 *The main features are delineated with a No. 3 sable brush loaded with Burnt Sienna. The details of the scarf and chair are picked up.*

5 *The fine detail of the portrait is rendered with a fine sable brush loaded with Vandyke Brown applied almost dry. The colour is heightened generally by delicate tints overlaid on the existing painting.*

6 *The drawing is refined with a fine sable brush.*

Portrait • *Critique*

The artist should have given more consideration to the viewpoint before starting work.

DEBORAH The artist has chosen a profile view of the model and this can be quite difficult to deal with in terms of the medium, since one must try to avoid creating an image that is too flat. The composition of this study is too symmetrical – it would have been better to include more of the foreground.

The delicacy of washes used on the features of the head are sensitive to the subject and work well on a hot-pressed paper.

The quality of light in the early stages has been lost to some extent

IAN In the early stages of this painting, we saw how the artist was concerned with basic abstract interlocking shapes of colour. It is well-composed – notice, for instance, how a single vertical stroke of Burnt Umber on the left-hand side serves to balance the loosely-ranged washes on the right. There is also an interesting interplay between hard-edged and soft washes of colour.

The quality of light in the early stages has to some extent been lost – though not to any great detriment to the painting as a whole.

This painting has been overworked in the final stage

ANTHONY This version of the portrait began as a monochromatic study in warm tints of Chrome and Ochre. It worked well in my view, in the penultimate stage – before the heavier tones were added to provide more definition. It is in the nature of watercolour painting that there are gains and losses at each stage. One might argue, for instance, that the addition of a darker tone to the coat enriches the colour of the scarf and the introduction of a green wash in the background complements the warmth of the wood panelling.

Animal Study

'FLORENCE'

Domestic animals have always been a source of interest to artists. The Egyptians, especially, produced magnificent murals depicting many varieties of birdlife.

Watercolour was used by Dürer to make animal studies – who can forget his wonderfully controlled watercolour painting of a hare, painted in 1502. My favourite paintings of cats are the watercolours produced by Gwen John (1876-1939) and, more recently, by the Scottish painter Elizabeth Blackadder.

Cats are vain creatures and they love to pose – but unfortunately not always at the exact time you want to paint them! There are essentially two ways of dealing with their unpredictable behaviour – one can either take into account that the cat is likely to move every few seconds and produce a kind of collage of rapid studies noting the movement itself or, alternatively, one can wait until they are more docile or asleep!

The cat we used in this project was quite indifferent to our attention but nevertheless tolerated our presence. Remember, even when you are painting an animal that is perfectly still, you should nevertheless try to paint it in such a way that suggests it is capable of movement.

Artist • Ian Potts

YELLOW OCHRE

PAYNES'S GREY

VIRIDIAN

VANDYKE BROWN

BURNT SIENNA

① *The paper is dampened and a succession of warm and cool washes are laid roughly following the form of the cat. The artist exercises control over each stage by laying the colour with tissue, allowing some areas to dry and blotting off other areas where the colour is too heavy. This process continues until the right tonal balance is achieved.*

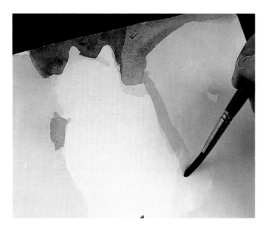

② *A No. 8 sable brush is loaded with a wash mixed from Vandyke Brown and Viridian – this lends more definition to the contour of the cat, and begins to suggest modelling of the form.*

③ *Greater definition is given to the head of the cat using a finer sable brush.*

④ *The final detail – the characteristic white whiskers are added using white body colour sparingly on a No. 1 sable brush.*

Artist • Anthony Colbert

❶ *A heavily-textured 300gsm / 140lb Bockingford (NOT) paper was used. The whites are masked out and a rich mix of Cadmium red with a touch of Ultramarine is used to isolate the form of the cat and provide a base colour for the carpet.*

❷ *The light ginger colour of the cat's fur is produced with a wash of Yellow Ochre and Burnt Sienna.*

❸ *The surface of the paper is dampened and darker ginger markings of the fur painted with Burnt Sienna.*

YELLOW OCHRE

CADMIUM RED

BURNT SIENNA

PAYNE'S GREY

FRENCH ULTRAMARINE BLUE

4 *Even darker markings are produced with a wash of Payne's Grey. Soft edges are diffused with a damp brush.*

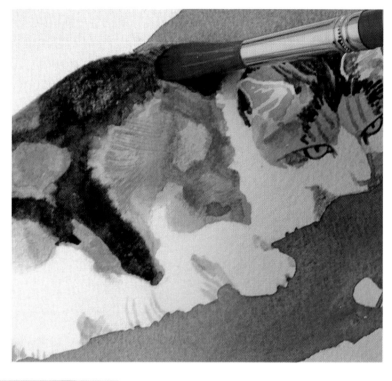

5 *With a dry No. 10 bristle brush, fur markings are added with a dry mix of Burnt Sienna and Yellow Ochre. The edges of the fur are softened with a clean, damp brush.*

6 *The decoration on the carpet is lifted out with a damp bristle brush and allowed to dry. Pale blue carpet decoration and cast shadows are added. Finally, the cat's whiskers are scratched out with a scalpel blade.*

Artist • Deborah Jameson

❶ *A rapid sketch is made directly onto a Saunders rough paper using a 3B pencil. A few washes of blue-black help to establish the form of the cat.*

❷ *Areas of shadow are rendered with further layered washes of the same blue-black.*

❸ *Blue-black is also used to pick out the detail of the chair cover.*

YELLOW OCHRE

INDIAN RED

CADMIUM RED

PAYNE'S GREY

INDIGO

4 *The red pattern of the carpet is introduced with a wash of Cadmium Red and Indian Red mixed in equal proportions.*

5 *The detail shows how the pattern of the carpet is hinted at with a few deft strokes of colour.*

6 *The tonal balance is adjusted by further washes. Dry brushwork produces details such as the animal's fur, and picks up here and there the intricacy of the patterned carpet and chair.*
Each layer of colour is allowed to dry thoroughly between each stage.

Animal Study • *Critique*

90

DEBORAH This is a fairly lucid handling of the subject, with all the elements jelling together quite well. The artist has managed to render detail without allowing the image to become stilted - the animal looks capable of movement, rather than being just a slavish Natural History illustration.

The animal is not too stilted - it looks capable of movement

ANTHONY This study is distinguished by the richness of the washes used. The textural qualities of the cat's fur have been handled well in terms of the medium used – a combination of wet-in-wet, broad dry brushwork and fine detail.

In the final stage of the painting, the added pattern of the carpet tends to distract rather too much from the main form of the cat. This could have been handled in a more selective way, or perhaps by making the tone of the carpet slightly darker.

Tone of carpet could be slightly darker

The main form has been lost to some extent

IAN A considerable amount of risk-taking has been involved in producing this painting - the artist's technique of applying and lifting-off washes in successive strokes demands concentration on maintaining a balance between lost and found shapes and a pre-determined knowledge of the effect that one wash will have when laid over another. There have been gains and losses in this painting – in the early stages it worked well in an overall way. In the final stage, however, the head of the cat is convincing, but the main form of the rest of the animal has been lost.

Interior

FARMHOUSE KITCHEN

'What I am after is the first impression... I want to show all one sees on first entering a room... what my eye takes in at first glance' (Pierre Bonnard, 1867-1947). One of the problems of attempting to produce a painting of one's own immediate domestic environment is over-familiarity. Bonnard had the ability to paint things freshly – as if he were seeing things for the first time. I find that one way of overcoming this problem is to cut a rectangle or square from an A4 sheet of card in order to view different parts of the room. By using a framing device in this way, a variety of compositional ideas emerge. Most artists taking up watercolour do so because it is a portable medium that can be used for painting landscape. The domestic interior might be thought of as a winter or 'bad-weather' subject – when Van Gogh was prevented by the *mistral* from painting outside, he turned to painting flowers and the humble arrangement of his few pieces of bedroom furniture. Yet we now think of these paintings as being among his most successful.

The kind of interior compositions which often work best are those where one can see from one room into another, and perhaps to a window beyond. There is an anticipatory element in such paintings which prevents them from being dull. For the Dutch artist, Vermeer (1632-75), the domestic interior was a subject of primary interest. He employed all kinds of visual devices to lead the eye towards the solitary figures which appear in his compositions. Chequered floor patterns, carpets and drapery, furniture, musical instruments – every element in his compositions served a particular purpose in supporting the central theme of the composition. As with still life, one has a degree of control in the way things are arranged. Shapes near and far need to be linked together in a way that is visually satisfying. It sometimes helps to make a series of preliminary sketches in pencil to sort out the basic formal elements of the composition. This will help you to decide what should be included and what should be excluded before you begin painting in watercolour.

Artist • Ian Potts

GAMBOGE YELLOW   YELLOW OCHRE   RAW UMBER   BURNT SIENNA   VANDYKE BROWN   VIRIDIAN   INDIGO

93

1 *The artist works directly with a broad flat sable brush onto dampened paper. Careful consideration is given to the main source of light through the open doorway and the way that the light is distributed on the objects on the table. Hues of colour merge wet-in-wet and cool into warm.*

3 *(Detail) A wash mixed from Cadmium Red and Yellow Ochre is applied with a piece of folded tissue.*

2 *The dark frame of the doorway is carefully blocked in with a wash made from varying proportions of Vandyke Brown, Indigo and Yellow Ochre. The same wash is diluted for shadows around the door and table. The various pots and fruit bowls are picked up with Burnt Sienna.*

5 *Final details, such as the coloured scarf on the chair, are added using a fine sable brush.*

4 *A darker wash of Vandyke Brown mixed with Raw Umber provides the shadows to the objects on the table.*

Artist • Anthony Colbert

94

❶ *Light objects on the table, such as the cheese cover, knife, plate and flowers, are masked out with masking fluid. A wash of pale Cadmium Yellow covers the whole of the interior. Lights are lifted with a dry brush and shadows are indicated wet-in-wet with Yellow Ochre.*

❷ *A second warm wash of Burnt Sienna is added – particularly on the table and door.*

❸ *Tones are established with browns and olive greens.*

CADMIUM YELLOW   YELLOW OCHRE   BURNT SIENNA   BURNT UMBER   CADMIUM RED   ALIZARIN CRIMSON   COBALT

95

5 *The painting is given greater depth by the addition of cast shadows on the table and other surfaces and recesses. Reflections and highlights are lifted out with a dry brush.*

4 *A range of washes closely related in tone are applied for shadows behind the door. Pale, cooler washes, used for the exterior, contrast with the warmth of the interior colours.*

6 *Fine details are added to flowers, fruit and to other objects on the table. Three brushes were used for this painting – a Hake $\frac{3}{4}$ inch, a Prolene 20 and a No. 8 sable.*

Artist • Deborah Jameson

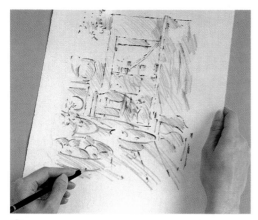

1 *From this viewpoint, the eye is lead across the kitchen table, through the open door towards a distant farmhouse. The main forms of the composition are denoted with a soft pencil on a Saunders rough paper.*

2 *A pale wash of Chrome Yellow separates the interior from the exterior and provides a base colour for successive washes.*

3 *A wash of Burnt Sienna is applied to the table and door and serves to underpin areas of shadow.*

CHROME YELLOW   NAPLES YELLOW   PAYNE'S GREY   BURNT SIENNA   ALIZARIN CRIMSON   INDIGO

4 *Darker hues are applied to enhance details in the painting. The tonal balance is built up using layering techniques.*

5 *A stronger wash of Payne's Grey is used to suggest the colour of the flint buildings seen in the distance.*

6 *The same wash is used to follow the form of objects on the table, the door frame and shadows created by the door itself.*

Interior • *Critique*

98

Good composition

IAN A well-composed painting which worked to particular advantage in the early stages, when the quality of light filtering through the doorway illuminated the objects on the table.

Something of this has been lost in the final stage when the tones have become more even, as further, darker washes have been laid over the more tentative washes of the earlier stage.

The painting nevertheless possesses a strong atmospheric quality, which is conducive to the subject.

Tones could have been darker to produce more contrast

ANTHONY The artist has obviously given a great deal of thought to the composition of this painting – he has deliberately distorted the perspective in order to invest the painting with more interest. The painting is distorted in the same way that a wide-angle lens would reproduce the scene, to suggest a greater feeling of being in the room, looking down at the table and out through the open door.

The doorway itself provides a useful device for separating warm and cool hues. The main criticism of this painting is that there could have been more tonal contrast on the interior, which in turn would have made the exterior appear even more brilliant.

Everything is too evenly disposed in terms of composition

DEBORAH Layered washes are handled well on the interior part of the painting but, as with the other two paintings, there is insufficient contrast between internal and external tonal values.

In terms of composition, the various elements are perhaps too evenly disposed – a different eye-level might have produced a better result.

Architecture

PARISH CHURCH

The indeterminate nature of landscape demands some point of reference – there are, of course, natural phenomena such as outcrops of rock, waterfalls, rivers and great forests. But more often than not, we look for some kind of reference to humanity. Farm buildings, isolated dwellings and churches can provide a point of interest in an otherwise featureless scene. Medieval builders gave great consideration to the selection of a suitable site for a building; moreover, they used locally quarried stone. This resulted in a much closer affinity between man-made and natural forms. In the U.S.A. and in other countries of the 'new world' there is often a fine tradition of timber-framed haylofts, barns, farmhouses and weatherboarded churches.

Architectural subjects demand contrast; the three-dimensional qualities of a building are best rendered by clearly-defined areas of light and shadow. It is important to consider the building in relation to the other elements within the field of vision – trees, paths and walls disposed at different levels lend a sense of scale to the painting and provide visual links between the various parts of the composition.

If your chosen subject happens to be a fairly ornate example of vernacular architecture, such as a castle or manor house with a great many windows and intricate stonework, the temptation to register every detail is bound to lead to failure. From whatever distance you are positioned from your subject, try to see the whole scene in terms of basic interlocking shapes. Be selective, by hinting at the textural quality of bricks, tiles and surrounding foliage. The success or failure of the painting will depend to some extent on the particular balance between form and structure. In watercolour, this means the parity between washes, which describe the broader areas of colour and tone, and the linear detail, which is expressed either by an underlying drawing or by dry brushwork.

Artist · Ian Potts

YELLOW OCHRE   BURNT SIENNA   BURNT UMBER   HOOKER'S GREEN   FRENCH ULTRAMARINE BLUE   VIRIDIAN   ALIZARIN CRIMSON

101

❶ *A base neutral wash mixed from Burnt Sienna with a touch of Ultramarine is laid with a wad of tissue onto a sheet of dampened Bockingford paper. When dry, further sombre colours are layered over the woodland area adjacent to the church.*

Pale washes of Viridian are laid over the sky area. A wash of French Ultramarine Blue, Burnt Umber and Yellow Ochre produce a pale green for the grass in the foreground of the scene.

❷ *Using both fine and medium sable brushes, details such as the spire of the church are added as a single wash of Grey Ochre. The tones of the distant foliage are heightened with layered washes.*

❸ *The tree on the left-hand side of the composition is loosely painted with a No. 8 sable brush loaded with Umber for the bark, which in turn is overlaid with Alizarin Crimson and Burnt Umber for shaded areas. Branches are added with a few deft strokes of the same colour.*

❹ *Architectural detailing is added to the church with a fine brush.*

Artist • Anthony Colbert

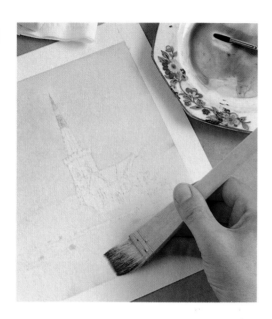

1 *Having traced down a fine line drawing of the main outlines of the composition, the church together with sapling stalks, tombstones and the church wall is masked out with masking fluid. A pale wash of Ultramarine Blue mixed with a little Alizarin Crimson provides an overall warm blue tone. The wash is made from top to bottom with a 1¾ inch Hake.*

2 *The lightest green is laid - mixed from Hooker's Green and a touch of Ultramarine. The wash is applied to the evergreens and to the foreground.*

3 *Using the same brush, the paper is dampened to produce a semicircle of tree haze behind and beside the church. A soft mix of Burnt Umber cooled with Indigo is dropped onto the dampened patches with a Hake that is almost dry. This effect produces a soft, warm, grey haze which suggests fine twigs and distant tree forms.*

NAPLES YELLOW   YELLOW OCHRE   BURNT UMBER   CADMIUM RED   HOOKER'S GREEN   FRENCH   INDIGO
ULTRAMARINE BLUE

5 *The masking fluid is removed. The light and dark areas of stonework on the church are added with varying strengths of Naples Yellow and grey.*

4 *Yellow Ochre and a touch of Burnt Umber are mixed together to produce a fairly strong warm tone for the tree trunk. This is overlaid with more Burnt Umber and Indigo with a dryer Hake, dragging the brush vertically across the wet trunk. At the same time, the brush is twisted slightly to throw out branches from the trunk into the dry paper. More detail is added to paths, shadows and trees, with a No. 4 sable.*

6 *Architectural detail is hinted at with a fine brush loaded with grey.*

Artist • Deborah Jameson

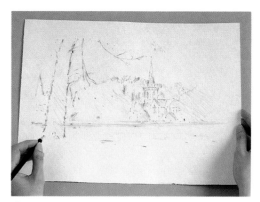

1 *The main forms of the composition are deliberately understated in pencil to allow the brush to produce the main drawing.*

2 *A pale wash mixed from Alizarin Crimson with a touch of Payne's Grey provides a neutral base for the painting, and serves to isolate the light on the façade of the church.*

3 *A single wash of Raw Sienna covers all the area of the painting except the sky. While still wet, the wash is lifted from the front of the church with a dry brush, to produce a paler tint.*

YELLOW OCHRE   HOOKER'S GREEN   PAYNE'S GREY   ALIZARIN CRIMSON   RAW SIENNA

105

4 *A green-umber wash, which is much darker in tone from the previous washes, is applied to define contrasts of light and shadow in the painting.*

5 *Successive washes of green-brown and violet are applied wet-in-wet to foliage. Hooker's Green is applied to the foreground and a paler wash of turquoise overlaid in the middle-distance. Finally, the architectural details and branches of trees are picked up using a fine dry brush technique.*

Architecture • *Critique*

Green–blue wash unsuited to subject

good handling of layered washes

IAN The apparent complexity of this scene has been successfully broken down into simple blocks of colour. The artist has exercised great restraint in selecting a few closely-related washes to convey the essential atmospheric qualities of an autumn day.

The sombre colours of the distant woodland contrast with the warmth of colour used for the church itself.

The wash laid over the sky is almost Viridian and, in my view, quite unsuited to the subject.

washes have been too overworked on trees

DEBORAH

There is a pervading atmosphere in this painting, which is suited to the subject and shows a good use of the medium. There has been much re-working of washes which has to some extent affected the transparency of the colour and produced an overall dullness.

good feeling for light

composition too stilted

ANTHONY There is a pleasant feeling of light in this painting – helped by the pale wash mixed from Ultramarine with a little Alizarin Crimson. Masking fluid has also been used effectively on the church.

One has the feeling, however, that the artist was too conscious of technique in this painting, albeit skilfully employed.

Townscape

STREET SCENE

When we see a church standing alone in the middle of a landscape, we experience it as a work of architecture. If, however, we see a street full of buildings of different proportions and architectural styles with groups of people scurrying to and fro up and down it, then we experience something quite different. Towns and cities are full of incidents which should arouse our visual interest.

The artist must always be ruled by what he sees – whilst a dilapidated building covered in advertisement posters may be an eyesore to the people who live in the vicinity, for the artist it might prove to be the most interesting part of his composition. Street furniture, traffic, advertisement hoardings and so on are woven together in a way that can invest a scene with a sense of drama. When one walks through a crowded street at a uniform speed everything is revealed in a series of sudden jerks and shifting perspectives. The human mind reacts to contrast, especially when old and new buildings are brought into juxtaposition.

In order to uncover the spirit of a town or city, it is necessary to look beyond the picturesque or the accepted 'guidebook' view of a place. Industrial suburbs can sometimes be infinitely more interesting visually than a smart shopping precinct. When visiting a city for the first time, I always like to wander off the beaten track down side streets and alleyways, in the hope of stumbling upon some unexpected vista.

Perhaps the biggest difference between working in landscape and a crowded city is that it is much harder to concentrate in the latter – especially when a continuous stream of people are passing by, some of whom will be curious to see exactly what you are up to! In a busy street you will probably find that you tend to draw more rapidly, and there will be little space to manage a box of watercolours and a pot of water. You will need to compromise, perhaps by producing brief notations rather than sustained studies. You might, for instance, produce a drawing and a series of colour notes which should provide enough information to enable you to produce a more complete study in the comfort of your own studio. If you are working from sketches, however, you will need to start the finished painting before your memory of the scene begins to fade.

Artist ▪ Ian Potts

PAYNE'S GREY   YELLOW OCHRE   INDIAN RED   BURNT SIENNA   COBALT   VIRIDIAN   ALIZARIN CRIMSON

1 *Using a flat sable brush, the main forms of the composition are blocked in. The ochre-red of the brickwork contrasts with the cooler blue-black tone of the road and the building on the left. Patches of colour suggesting windows and doors are overlaid when the first washes are dry.*

2 *The darker tones are heightened by additional washes overlaid on some areas, and blotted off elsewhere with a paper towel.*

3 *Further architectural detail is suggested by simple blocks of ochre-brown and brick red.*

4 *The group of figures in the middle-distance are now introduced using a No. 4 sable and simple blocks of colour.*

5 *The lettering on the surface of the road is reversed-out of the colour previously laid, using the tip of a cotton bud dipped in water.*

Artist • Anthony Colbert

110

❶ *A detailed preliminary drawing of the entire composition is made on tracing paper.*

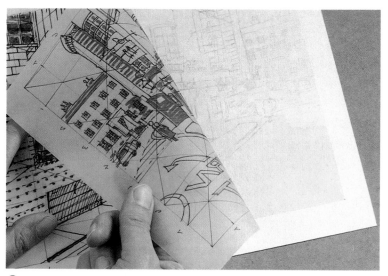

❷ *Using a Dalon 1½ inch brush, two washes of Cadmium red provide a base for the painting – a third wash is added to the road. When dry, the main architectural details are traced-down.*

❸ *The distant house is painted in with Indigo for the roof and windows. Cadmium Yellow is added for the brickwork. A base yellow is added to fascia boards and signs.*

CADMIUM YELLOW   CADMIUM RED   BURNT UMBER   INDIGO   COBALT   ALIZARIN CRIMSON

4 *A cool wash of Indigo and a touch of Cobalt Blue is added to the stone wall with a dragged Dalon brush. A second wash is added to slates.*

5 *The brickwork is dealt with by using one or two strokes with a Dalon $\frac{1}{4}$ inch - warm with yellow, cool with Ultramarine - dropped in while still damp. Blue stipple is added to the flint wall using a No. 8 sable, also lifting and adding colour to the slates.*

Cadmium Red is added to the pub sign.

A mix of Indigo and Burnt Umber is added to the pub fascia and window box.

The warm and cool tones of the paving are established with a Dalon $\frac{1}{2}$ inch and shadows are introduced.

6 *The lettering on the road is masked out. Two successive washes of Indigo mixed with a little Burnt Umber are then overlaid. A stronger wash of Light Red is added to the shaded side of the door, window and doorframes.*

Details are painted with a No. 4 sable using warm darks mixed with Burnt Umber and cool darks mixed with blue.

Artist • Deborah Jameson

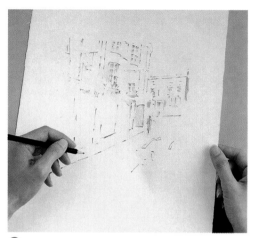

1 *The main architectural details – seen in perspective – are lightly suggested with a soft (2B) pencil on Bockingford 190gsm / 90lb (NOT) paper.*

2 *A wash of Payne's Grey is first laid over the whole area of the street scene, using a broad Chinese brush.*

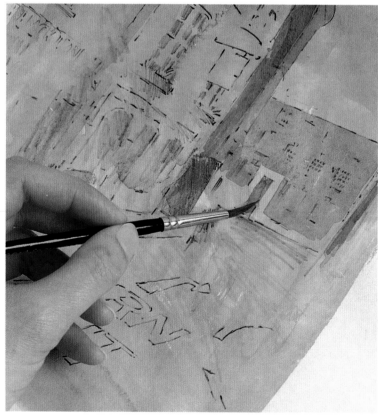

3 *When the first wash has dried, a pale wash of Burnt Sienna is used to depict brickwork on buildings at the far end of the street and as a more delicate wash over the building in the foreground.*

NAPLES YELLOW

PAYNE'S GREY

BURNT SIENNA

ALIZARIN CRIMSON

FRENCH
ULTRAMARINE BLUE

BURNT UMBER

113

4 *A stronger wash of Payne's Grey is overlaid on the road surface, loosely following the contours of the lettering and other road markings. Washes of the same colour define shadows.*

5 *A wash of mauve is added to suggest slates and flints on the building in the foreground.*

6 *The tonal balance is built up, but without being overstated or too sharply defined.*

Townscape • *Critique*

good use of contrasting tones

IAN Here the artist has managed to invest an otherwise dull street scene with an almost Mediterranean light! This has something to do with both the choice and relationship of the colours used.

Architectural detail has been handled with economy, using broad washes overlaid with selected details such as windows and doors added with a fine brush.

Most of the interest is confined to the middle-distance - this might have been overcome by, for instance, including the head and shoulders of a figure in the foreground.

Good composition

Architectural detail handled well

ANTHONY One gets a real sense of the different architectural styles of the street in this painting – there has been a great deal of attention to detail without over-loading the painting with superfluous information. The light is fairly even, without too much contrast – and, in fact, this leads one to suggest that the choice of season, and time of day, could be quite critical to producing a satisfactory study of this subject.

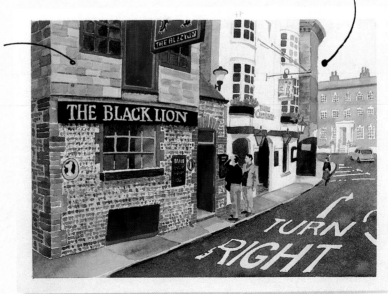

Light is too even

The white surface of the paper could have been used to better effect

DEBORAH This watercolour sketch has obviously been rapidly executed – the artist here is concerned with notation rather than with a prolonged study of architectural detail.

Again, the light is rather even – the white surface of the paper could have been used to better effect. Nevertheless, the atmospheric qualities are appropriate to the subject.

Landscape

RED BARNS

There are now few parts of our planet that man has not had some part in shaping – forests have been cleared and replanted, valleys flooded to create reservoirs, the land ploughed and tilled to grow crops and boundaries constructed to enclose pasture roads and railways built to link small communities to towns and cities. In fact, the whole history of human development is imprinted in the land itself.

Nostalgia is often the driving force behind landscape painting – our attachment to a vanishing past is generally held to be a mark of our inability to see the shape of the present. Most contemporary landscape paintings, therefore, refer to the past rather than the present. Much depends, of course, on where one happens to be living – if, for example, you happen to be living in a suburb of Melbourne, Australia, or on an American farm such as the one chosen for this project, you will have a totally different outlook to an artist living in northern Europe. An artist usually works best on his own 'patch' – although sometimes he has to travel around the world to discover simple truth.

Wherever you happen to live, you will need to take account of the particular terrain and geology of the region and to discover how best you can express those qualities in watercolour. Again, climate will be an important factor – the mood and atmosphere created by the equable climate of northern Europe is quite different from the clarity of light that can be experienced in countries in the southern hemisphere.

Choosing the right time of day and the right season for your subject is also important. It sometimes happens that we see a place under particular conditions of light, at a certain time of day, only to discover when we return to paint the scene a day or so later that it looks quite different. If we are patient, however, we will discover exactly the right time of day that is most suited to the subject. In a warm southern climate, the light may be too intense except in early morning or towards dusk, whereas the intrinsic qualities of a northern mountainous region might look best in rain or snow.

Artist • Ian Potts

INDIAN RED   RAW UMBER   BURNT SIENNA   COBALT   INDIGO   BURNT UMBER   VIRIDIAN

117

① *A warm neutral wash is laid with tissue on dampened paper and blotted off again in the area of the sky, before being allowed to dry. A grainy wash of Viridian mixed with Cobalt Blue is applied over the sky and blotted off on the silos and barn roofs. The rich red colour of the barns is expressed with a single blocking shape of Indian Red and Raw Umber.*
The earth colour extends from the middle-distance to the foreground.

② *The dark, cylindrical shapes of the silos are painted in with a No. 8 sable brush, loaded with a wash made from equal proportions of Cobalt Blue and Vandyke Brown with a touch of Indian Red. The darker tones are dragged over the field area with a dry brush.*

③ *Highlights and shadows are introduced with a fine sable brush.*

④ *The earth colour is enriched with another wash mixed from Burnt Umber, Vandyke Brown and a touch of Indian Red.*
While still wet, certain passages are blotted off with a paper towel.

Artist ◦ Anthony Colbert

1 *The artist decided to paint the subject at dusk in order to heighten the drama of the composition. He began by making a rough preliminary study in charcoal. After lightly drawing in the main features of the composition, the roofs, tops of silos and crops are masked out. A warm wash of light red is added to the skyline – diffused upwards with a damp brush.*

2 *The surface of the paper is moistened and the sky brushed in with a mix of Prussian Blue and Indigo. This in turn is made lighter towards the skyline with a damp brush.*

3 *The sky is masked out with film, leaving the silos and barn walls free. Light red is brushed and spattered into the barn walls and Naples Yellow used as a base for the crops.*

NAPLES YELLOW

CADMIUM RED

HOOKER'S GREEN

INDIGO

PRUSSIAN BLUE

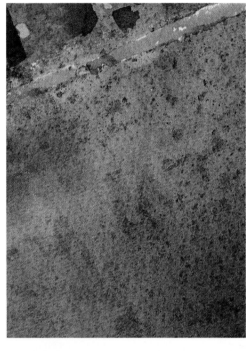

5 *The tone of the barn is moderated with a wash of dark Prussian Blue and Indigo.*

4 *A mixture of Prussian Blue and Indigo are added quickly with a Hake - the board is rocked slightly to bring out the grain of the paper. Indigo is spattered using a toothbrush to add texture.*

6 *All the masks are removed. The skyline and tree forms are added. Posts and roof angles are reduced with cool Indigo. The top crop line is indicated with a wash of Hooker's Green. Finally, a blue-black ink is used to darken the silo on the extreme left and to suggest the tree behind.*

Artist • Deborah Jameson

1 *A Bockingford CP (NOT) surface paper has been selected. The outline of the barns and silos are registered with a 2B pencil.*

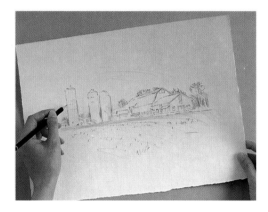

2 *French Ultramarine is mixed together with just a touch of Alizarin Crimson to produce the first overall wash.*

3 *Burnt Sienna and Raw Umber produce the next wash to be applied, which in turn produces a green-grey colour when laid over the existing blue.*

BURNT SIENNA   RAW UMBER   BURNT UMBER   INDIAN RED   FRENCH
ULTRAMARINE BLUE   ALIZARIN CRIMSON

5 *French Ultramarine is used to provide tonal contrast and, when used dryly, to pick out detail on the buildings, trees and field.*

4 *The distinctive colour of the barn is produced by applying a wash of Indian Red – which also adds warmth to the earth colour in the foreground. A second wash of blue is applied to the sky.*

6 *A darker blue-black tone is added to the silos.*

Landscape • *Critique*

Good unity of tone

ANTHONY In this version, the artist has elected to paint the scene at dusk, when colour values are radically different – especially on the barns where the local colour is reduced by shadow. Colours are much more muted and unified at this time of day, so that the image tends to read as a single, monochromatic statement.

Wet-in-wet techniques have been used to good effect in the foreground and provide a foil to the stark silhouettes of the barns and silos.

wet-in-wet technique used to advantage

IAN The rich terracotta colour of the barns supplements the blue-green wash used for the sky.

Softer washes of red-umber and red-brown occupy almost two thirds of the picture plane. The sentinel silos on the left-hand side of the painting serve to punctuate a predominantly horizontal composition. One has the sense that the artist has enjoyed painting a scene which has allowed him to exploit such unusual colour relationships.

Rich colour contrast between sky, barns and cabin.

DEBORAH This is a fairly 'matter-of-fact' rendering of the subject which makes no attempt to seduce the viewer with rich colour or with the techniques used.

In terms of composition, everything is too evenly balanced and it might have been better to include more of the foreground or, conversely, more of the sky.

Composition too evenly balanced

Seascape

NEWHAVEN HARBOUR

On the face of it, a seascape should be the easiest of all subjects to tackle – there are few elements to contend with and a single wash of colour for the sea and sky should suffice to produce a harmonious composition. In my experience, however, a seascape can be one of the most demanding of all subjects; precisely because there are few elements, it requires the most careful judgement and restraint.

Composition is critical – particularly the position of the horizon line which can determine the emphasis given to sky or sea. Even on a cloudless day, the light and mood of a seascape can change rapidly. The underlying composition, therefore, needs to be firmly established. A low horizon in your composition would make the sky the key note of the whole painting. Conversely, a horizon line pitched high in your painting would lead one to concentrate on the sea. If the horizon is placed equidistant between sea and sky, there needs to be some other element which offers contrast to the symmetry of the composition. Of course, the horizon might be lost by a sea mist or by the quality of light on a hazy summer's day.

Watercolour is eminently suited to the evocation of such atmospheric qualities. A series of washes are usually needed to render the vaporous atmosphere of a seascape convincingly – the tonal strength of the painting should be allowed to accrue by laying three or four pale washes over one another, rather than by trying to achieve the same effect with a single wash. The near-abstract qualities of the painting can be given added richness by careful tonal contrast.

The sea has many moods, particularly in the northern hemisphere where in winter it can change from hour to hour. Not many artists, I suspect, would want to follow Turner's example by having themselves strapped to the mast of a ship in order to record directly a storm at sea!

Before starting a finished painting, you might find it useful to make some preliminary studies in your sketchbook. Look intently at the way that one wave folds over another on an incoming tide. Notice how patterns are created by the movement of the water itself and try different movements with your loaded brush to capture these qualities.

Artist • Ian Potts

CADMIUM ORANGE   YELLOW OCHRE   VIRIDIAN   INDIGO   FRENCH
ULTRAMARINE BLUE   COBALT

125

1 *The artist has used the full page of an A3 sketchbook for this painting. Having first sponged the surface of the paper to soften the size content, he has applied a series of washes – some laid wet-in-wet, others allowed to dry before further layering. All the main features of the composition are in place at this stage – although everything is understated and atmospheric.*

2 *A fine sable brush and a broader flat brush are now used to define more sharply the folds in the waves.*

Washes of green-blue, such as Viridian, contrast with red-blues, such as Ultramarine.

3 *The wooden jetty is included at this stage, using a No. 8 sable.*

4 *A wash of Cadmium Orange applied with a Hake brush provides a warm tone above the horizon.*

Artist · Anthony Colbert

1 *A pale line drawing of the composition is traced-down onto a sheet of Arches 300gsm / 140lb (NOT) paper.*

The cliffs, lighthouse and sails are stopped out with masking fluid.

2 *The paper is dampened with a Dalon 1½ inch brush just above the horizon. A generous wash of Burnt Sienna is laid from right to left with a Prolene 20 brush.*

3 *The rest of the sky area is lightly dampened and a pale wash of Cerulean Blue is laid with a Hake 3 inch. The wash is carried on below the horizon where the paper is dry.*

BURNT SIENNA   BURNT UMBER   ALIZARIN CRIMSON   FRENCH ULTAMARINE BLUE   INDIGO   CERULEAN BLUE

4 *While the first wash is still wet, a second wash mixed from Ultramarine, Indigo and a touch of Alizarin Crimson is brushed upwards from the headland, with a ³⁄₄ inch Hake. A cloudburst is established, as well as other cloud forms. A darker tone of Indigo reinforces the overhead raincloud and its shade in the foreground.*

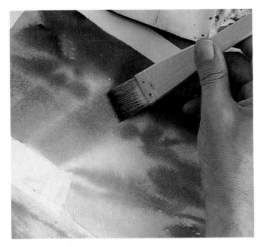

5 *The same brush is rinsed to take up a mix of Burnt Sienna and Ultramarine for the shaded headland and grassland.*
A similar mix of colour is used for the pier, dragging the colour from right to left with a No. 8 bristle. A ruler is used as a guide for the brush ferrule to produce a hard edge to the wash.

6 *The masking fluid is removed. The structure of the pier is made more convincing with a darker monochromatic wash applied with a flat Dalon ¹⁄₂ inch. The same brush is used to paint the lighthouse structure. Finally, a touch of light orange complements the predominantly blue hue of the painting.*

Artist • Deborah Jameson

128

1 *The first stage of the painting is carried out with a fine No. 3 sable brush loaded with a wash of Cobalt Blue. The paper used is a Waterford rough surface.*

2 *A broader brush is used to mop up a copious supply of Cobalt mixed with Indigo and lay it down in one decisive action – allowing the white of the paper to show through on the cliffs, pier and boat.*

3 *A second, more intense blue is overlaid when the first is dry. Additionally, a neutral green (mixed from Ochre Yellow and Cerulean Blue) is applied to the distant landscape. The wooden structure of the pier is brushed in with Burnt Sienna.*

YELLOW OCHRE   PAYNE'S GREY   COBALT   INDIGO   ALIZARIN CRIMSON   CERULEAN BLUE

129

4 *Two further washes of blue are overlaid at this stage – a Cerulean Blue influences the wash applied to the sea.*

5 *A touch of Alizarin Crimson is added to the hull of the sailing boat.*

6 *Most of the work in the final stage of the painting is concentrated on the structure of the pier and lighthouse. The folds in the waves are picked up with short, dry brushstrokes and some spatterwork is added. Undulating shadows are added to the waves with a medium sable and Indigo.*

Seascape • *Critique*

DEBORAH The long wooden jetty in this painting acts as a kind of balance in visual terms between the lighthouse and the yacht.

A change of scale might have benefited the composition – by painting the yacht larger, for instance.

The contrasting washes of warm and cool blues work well, as does the restrained use of colour elsewhere in the painting.

getting nearer to the subject or a change of scale might have been of benefit to this painting

ANTHONY There is a sense of drama in this painting which is absent in the others. This is due in part to the treatment of the sky, which occupies three-quarters of the total area of the painting.

The yacht and lighthouse are placed roughly on a Golden Section ratio of 5:3 and this works well. One might argue that the treatment of the surface of the sea itself is perhaps too opaque – but, on the other hand, in chalkland regions the colours are often modified by the presence of chalk on the headland and on the sea-bed.

Good sense of drama in the handling of this painting

IAN The central part of this seascape composition works very well. The relationship of the single yacht to the horizontal harbour wall and the chalk cliffs emerging from the mist recall the seascapes of Turner.

The loosely-painted wooden piles on the right-hand side of the composition, however, serve only to distract from the central core of the painting and do not contribute much to the composition as a whole.

Again, the colour values are more akin to a southerly climate than to the northern hemisphere!

wooden piles distract from the core of the composition

Change Of Scene

ITALIAN LANDSCAPE

The travelling artist needs to take account of the fact that, in the process of searching for a suitable subject, he is likely to have to do a lot of walking and climbing to different levels. A certain amount of preparation beforehand can therefore help to ease the burden of carrying around too much cumbersome equipment. Everything needs to be kept to a minimum – a lightweight shoulderbag might contain a box of watercolours, pencils and brushes (in a protective tube), plastic waterpots (2), waterbottles, paper towels and a spiral-bound sketchbook or a variety of watercolour papers clipped to a supporting sheet of hardboard. Protective clothing is also necessary especially if, like me, you find it difficult to judge the weather pattern in another country. It is one thing to be walking around for a subject to paint but, having found it, you might be sitting still for two or three hours at a time. Climate has a bearing on everything and, in my experience, it is rare to find conditions that are perfect for painting. It may be too hot, too cold, windy or wet and, having found your subject, you may have chosen the wrong time of day. In mountainous regions such as Switzerland, for instance, one side of the valley might be in shadow for most of the day.

The subject selected for this project is the gentle, undulating countryside of Tuscany in central Italy. It is a scene which represents the classical ideal in landscape painting and one which is relatively unchanged since the time of Simone Martini (c.1285-1344) and Piero della Francesca (c.1410/20-92). Cypress trees provide dark sentinels which punctuate the predominantly horizontal forms of this wine-growing area. The artists worked early in the morning, at that time of day when the mist has cleared and the sun has not yet risen above the hills. The whole scene is invested with a sense of mystery as buildings and distant forms are not clearly defined. The narrow road leads the eye from the foreground towards barely perceived farm buildings on a distant hill.

Artist · Ian Potts

BURNT SIENNA

ALIZARIN CRIMSON

VANDYKE BROWN

HOOKER'S GREEN

COBALT

FRENCH
ULTRAMARINE BLUE

❶ *An A3 Bockingford spiral-bound sketchbook has been used vertically rather than horizontally to make the composition more interesting.*

A much-diluted warm ochre-brown wash has been laid over the whole page with tissue and allowed to dry. Further colours have been applied wet-in-wet and merging from blue-grey on the horizon to purple-grey in the fore-ground. Details on the horizon have been added using a much finer sable brush.

❷ *Tonal contrasts are now firmly established – a line of cypress trees in the middle-distance is painted in as the strongest tone with a mix of green-brown.*

Colours in the foreground are intensified by a sequence of layered washes – mauve-grey made from Alizarin Crimson, Ultramarine and a touch of Burnt Sienna. A blue-green wash made from Cerulean Blue and Hooker's Green is overlaid on the grass verges.

❸ *Tonal contrasts are further heightened with richer washes of the previous colours used. Colour is applied with tissue to broader areas, such as the road surface, and with a No. 8 sable brush for more sharply-defined forms such as trees, grass and shadows. The painting has now more depth tonally.*

❹ *The darkest tone of the painting – a near black – is mixed from Alizarin Crimson, Vandyke Brown and Ultramarine. This is painted over the cypress trees in the middle-distance and on the road surface in the fore-ground. Those parts of the colour which appear too heavy tonally are blotted off again while the colour is still wet.*

Artist • Anthony Colbert

1 *A base wash of Alizarin Crimson mixed with Raw Sienna covers the whole area. When dry, a second wash of the same mix follows the contours on the horizon and continues covering the middle-distance and foreground.*

2 *A very pale wash of Prussian Blue helps to intensify the tone of the hills, buildings and trees.*

3 *A stronger wash of Indigo with Yellow Ochre and Burnt Sienna is laid on trees and establishes shadows and furrows in the fields.*

The paper is dampened and the track and verges picked out with a wash of Indigo and Cobalt Blue. The same wash is allowed to fade into the foreground of the road.

NAPLES YELLOW YELLOW OCHRE BURNT SIENNA BURNT UMBER INDIGO ALIZARIN CRIMSON PRUSSIAN BLACK

4 *The colour around the verge is lifted and softened to take a wash of Burnt Sienna. Trees in the middle-distance are made darker. Flowers and stones in the foreground are masked out.*

5 *The dark cypress tree is brought up to full strength. Damp and dry brush strokes are used in the foreground along the verge. Masking fluid is removed and flowers and stones painted in with Naples Yellow, Burnt Umber and Burnt Sienna.*

135

6 *This detail shows how the bristles of a Prolene 20 brush are flayed between finger and thumb to drag colour across scrubland.*

Artist • Deborah Jameson

136

❶ *The main forms of the landscape are drawn with a soft pencil on a hot-pressed sheet of watercolour paper.*

❷ *A warm wash mixed from Cadmium Orange and Naples Yellow is brushed over the whole area of the composition with a large Chinese brush.*

❸ *A wash of Payne's Grey is applied at this stage, to produce an even tone that is without contrast.*

NAPLES YELLOW   BURNT SIENNA   PAYNE'S GREY CADMIUM ORANGE   FRENCH
ULTRAMARINE BLUE

4 *The landscape forms are heightened with a wash mixed from Burnt Sienna and Naples Yellow. A green-brown wash is also applied to the cypress trees in the middle-distance.*

5 *A rich, olive-coloured wash is made from Payne's Grey, Yellow Ochre and Prussian Blue. This is used fairly solidly on the trees and as a wash on the landscape.*

A Change Of Scene • *Critique*

IAN The early stages of this painting revealed exquisite qualities of light – the radiance of which has been lost to some extent in the final painting.

One has the feeling that the artist felt constrained by the size of the paper on which he was working – his technique of laying on colour in broad washes might perhaps have worked better on a larger format.

In purely abstract terms, this painting works very well – it is rather like looking at a detail from a larger painting.

Radiance of light in early stages has been lost

Good feeling for light

ANTHONY This painting demonstrates a mature handling of the medium – the quality of diffused sunlight is particularly effective. One has the impression of a heat-haze in the distance – dust-laden, rather than dull and misty.

It is also a well-composed painting in which the cypress trees seem to punctuate the landscape at intervals which are critical to the visual balance of the painting.

Good Composition

Good tonal control

There could have been more graduated tones

DEBORAH This painting also conveys a feeling of diffused sunlight, although the brushwork is more loosely handled.

The choice of a few washes which are closely related in tone and colour works to advantage for this subject. There could have been even more graduation of tone from light to dark and from sky to foreground.

Glossary

A

ALLA PRIMA

Painting directly onto a support in a single session, without any preliminary underpainting or drawing.

AQUARELLE

Alternative generic name for watercolour. Also brand name for water-soluble coloured pencils.

ATMOSPHERE

Relates to the suggested recession in a painting, achieved by changes in tone and colour between the foreground and background.

B

BLENDING

Merging colours together with a brush.

BODY COLOUR

Essentially, white gouache. Can also refer to watercolour paint mixed with white gouache to make it opaque.

C

CALLIGRAPHIC

A term which refers to a cursive linear mark.

CHARCOAL

Sticks for drawing made from charred willow or vine twigs.

COMPLEMENTARY COLOURS

Complementary colours are found opposite each other on the colour wheel. A colour is complementary to the colour with which it contrasts most strongly, such as red with green.

COMPOSITION

The satisfactory disposition of all the related elements in a painting.

CROSS-HATCHING

A means of creating tone with a pen or pencil using layers of criss-cross parallel lines.

D

DRAWING IN

The initial statement of the drawing prior to painting.

DRY BRUSH

A technique in which excess water is squeezed out of the brush. This leaves a residue of dry pigment, which is then applied to the surface of the paper, creating a textured broken line.

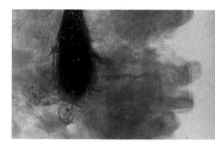

F

FERRULE

The metal part of the brush which binds the hair to the wooden handle.

FORM

A term which refers to the three-dimensional appearance of a shape.

FILLER

Pigment-like material usually white in colour – e.g. chalk. Used in the manufacture of gouache.

FUGITIVE

Used to describe colours that are liable to fade under strong light or in the course of time.

G

GOUACHE
An opaque water-soluble paint. Sometimes called body colour.

GRAIN
Refers to the direction of the fibres in machine-made papers. Handmade papers have no directional grains. The different surface qualities of watercolour paper is determined by the texture of the felts through which it is pressed or 'couched'. Hot-pressed paper is additionally pressed through heated rollers to produce a smooth surface.

GRAPHITE
A form of carbon used in the 'lead' for pencil manufacture.

GUM ARABIC
In purest form, the sap produced by acacia trees; used as a binding medium in watercolours.

H

HALF-TONE
A tone mid-way between black and white, or the strength between the lightest and darkest tone.

HUE
The colour, rather than the tone, of a pigment or object.

L

LOCAL COLOUR
The actual colour of an object, such as the red of an apple, rather than a colour which is modified by light or shadow.

M

MEDIUM
The medium is (a) the type of material used to produce a drawing or painting e.g. charcoal, pastel, watercolour, oil, etc. or (b) a substance blended with paint to thicken, thin, or dry the paint.

MODELLING
Expressing the volume and solidity of an object by light and shade.

MONOCHROME
Refers to a painting produced with a single colour, gradations of colour, or in black and white.

142

 N

NOT

A term used to describe the surface quality of watercolour papers – between hot-pressed and rough.

 O

OPAQUE

Describes the density of paint. Not transparent.

 P

PALETTE

A dish or tray on which colours are mixed – made from wood, metal or china. Also refers to the range of colours selected individually by the artist.

PERSPECTIVE

A means of recreating the illusion of three dimensions when painting on a two-dimensional surface. Linear perspective makes use of parallel lines which converge on a vanishing point. Aerial perspective suggests distance by the use of tone.

PICTURE PLANE

An imaginary transparent vertical screen between the artist and the subject. It is set at the distance from the artist where the drawing is intended to begin.

PIGMENT

The coloured matter of paint originally derived from plants, animal, vegetable and mineral products. Generally synthesized chemically in paint manufacture.

 R

RESIST

A term which refers to the use in watercolour painting of wax and masking fluid which are both water resistant.

 S

SIZE

A weak solution of any form of glue. In the manufacture of watercolour papers, a size is applied to impregnate the surface and control the degree of absorbency. The size usual for paper is traditionally made from gelatine with alum dissolved in alkalis.

SPATTER

A means of creating a texture of flecked particles of coloured paint by dragging the bristles of the brush against the blunt edge of a knife.

SUPPORT

The surface on which the painting is made (canvas, wood, paper, etc.).

 T

TONE

The light and dark value of a colour; for example, pale red is the same tone as pale ochre but both are lighter in tone than dark brown.

 W

WASH

Diluted watercolour applied to the surface of paper. Dries as a thin transparent film of colour.

WATERCOLOUR

Coloured pigment bound in gum arabic, water-soluble.

WET-IN-WET

A watercolour technique which allows colours to merge randomly whilst still wet.

Index

143

Index